Helping with Enquiries:

Tackling Crime Effectively

LONDON: HMSO

Printed in the UK for the Audit Commission at College Hill Press
ISBN 011 886 101 8

London : HMSO

Audit Commission, Police Paper No.12, 1993

Front cover: with thanks to Thames Television and 'The Bill'

Preface

The Audit Commission produced its first Police Paper in 1988, on the subject of administrative support for police officers. Other papers followed, concentrating on support functions such as fingerprinting and training. Later papers addressed strategic management issues such as financial devolution and territorial structure.

The present report on crime management looks at an activity which many people view as the primary role of the police. But the fight against crime is the responsibility not just of the police but also of government, business and each individual citizen. The report's recommendations reflect this, although they concentrate upon the measures which the police can adopt to improve current levels of performance.

The fieldwork for the study was carried out in police forces of different sizes and in different parts of the country. Five forces were examined across the board and in depth, whilst eight others were visited to look at specific aspects of crime management such as fingerprinting, crime prevention and the use of crime desks. Discussions were also held with officers from a large number of other forces. This fieldwork was supplemented by documentary research, data analysis, a survey of victims of crime and a questionnaire sent to all provincial police forces. Some examples of good practice by named forces are cited in the report; this is for purposes of illustration and does not imply that only these forces have implemented the procedures noted.

The study team benefited from the advice of the Home Office Police Department, Her Majesty's Inspectorate of Constabulary, the Crime Committee of ACPO and discussions with the Superintendents' Association and the Police Federation. Structured contributions were made by an advisory panel and a study working group (see Appendix 1 for membership). Many individual officers also contributed ideas and information upon which many of the findings are based. The Commission is grateful to all contributors, and in particular the five forces which hosted the in-depth fieldwork. As always, responsibility for the conclusions reached in this paper is that of the Commission alone.

The study team comprised Kate Flannery and Laura Hawksworth from the Local Government Studies Directorate, and Chris Rockey, seconded from the District Audit Service, under the direction of Steve Evans. Detective Superintendent John Hynes was seconded from Hampshire Constabulary to assist with the study and Inspector Nigel Arnold from Avon and Somerset Constabulary undertook a short attachment. Other contributions were made by Vanessa Couchman, Steve Jackson, Rob Mathie, Catherine Purcell and Andy Taylor, all from the District Audit Service.

The issues covered in this paper will be reviewed by local auditors at individual police forces in England and Wales in 1994, except the Metropolitan Police, which is not audited by the Commission's appointed auditors.

Table of Contents

Summary

The level of recorded crime in England and Wales rose by 74% in the decade to 1992, whilst the proportion of crimes detected (cleared up) by the police has declined during this period from 37% to 26%. These headline figures would, if they were robust measures of performance, suggest a deterioration in the effectiveness of the police.

However, the number of police officers rose in that period by only 6%, and therefore the number of crimes handled by each police officer has risen dramatically since 1982. Police productivity – as gauged by the number of clear-ups per officer – has increased, but not enough to keep pace with rising levels of crime. If crime levels rise to those of some other developed countries, then the proportion of crimes cleared up will continue to decline unless forces adopt an integrated approach based on the good practices currently used in isolation by some forces.

The police response to crime must be seen within the context of the criminal justice system as a whole. There needs to be a recognition of the limited impact that police actions can have upon the causes of crime or upon the prosecution, sentencing and rehabilitation of offenders. However, the police carry the main responsibility for the investigation of crime and, in partnership with others, have substantial responsibility for crime prevention.

The police and the rest of the criminal justice system are locked into a vicious circle in which the volume of crime threatens to become overwhelming and distracts the police from taking a proactive approach which would secure more detections and help stem the growth in crime. The problems are not ones of commitment or competence on the part of individual officers, nor is there a lack of recognition that changes are needed. Individual forces have tackled particular aspects of all the problems, but what is needed is for forces to step back and look at crime investigation in the round. There are three main areas that must be tackled:

— *developing integrated strategies which clarify roles and accountabilities.* Forces should clarify what share of resources should be devoted to crime management (i.e. prevention and investigation of crime). There is scope for increasing this share by concentrating more on core policing functions – which need to be defined by government – civilianising more posts and reducing management overheads. The role of criminal investigation departments (CID) needs new definition as forces restructure and devolve operational responsibility to front-line commanders. The crimes assigned to detectives for investigation should be of a seriousness and complexity which require their expertise, leaving less serious crime to be investigated by uniformed officers, but to higher standards than are currently achieved;

— *making the best use of resources.* The police try hard to direct resources efficiently but, as in most organisations, there is room for improvement. The initial response to crime reports, particularly burglaries, can involve duplication of effort, which puts already strained resources under greater pressure. Forces should consider the establishment of crime desks, which handle all calls about crime and assess whether there is a need for further investigation. Some forces may find it appropriate to expand the concept into a crime management unit

1

which drives the entire response to, and investigation of, crime at the local level. There is a need in some forces for more effective prioritisation of cases, and generally more rigorous supervision by sergeants of both the process of investigation and the end product. Valuable police time is absorbed by paperwork and administrative tasks. Measures should be taken by forces themselves *and* other agencies in the criminal justice system to alleviate this burden. Management information systems have improved markedly but need further development to ensure there is an adequate information base for decision-making;

— *targeting the criminals rather than responding to crime incidents.* A consequence of rising workload, some duplication of effort and the paperwork burden is that the focus of detectives' work is upon the crime incident rather than the criminal. This draws them away from the proactive work needed to apprehend those prolific criminals who generate much of the police workload and impose such damage upon communities. A change in emphasis away from reaction to crime incidents towards strategies for crime reduction and targeting of prolific offenders is needed, although without sacrificing attention to the victims of crime. Proactive work is driven by intelligence information, but in many forces the intelligence function is inadequately equipped with technology and understaffed. Informants, a highly cost-effective source of detections, are under-used.

The police alone cannot tackle the rise in crime. The government, other agencies in the criminal justice system and individual citizens must all play their part. The public need to recognise that whilst putting 'more bobbies on the beat' may help to assuage the fear of crime, it is not effective as a means of detecting crime. But by adopting the recommendations in this report the police can help to prevent crime and raise clear-up levels significantly, which itself will help to deter would-be criminals. The ultimate prize for the police, the criminal justice system and society is to break out of the current vicious circle into a virtuous circle in which the crime rate could be brought under control.

Introduction

1. Conventional crime statistics show the number of incidents reported to the police, the number which are formally recorded as crimes and the number of crimes which are cleared up. The trends exposed by these statistics are worrying. In 1992 there were 5.4 million crimes[1] recorded by the police in England and Wales, equivalent to 620 per hour. This represents a 74% increase since 1982, continuing a significant growth in recorded crime over many decades (Exhibit 1).

Exhibit 1
TOTAL RECORDED CRIME IN ENGLAND AND WALES 1901-1992
Recorded crime has risen significantly over many decades...

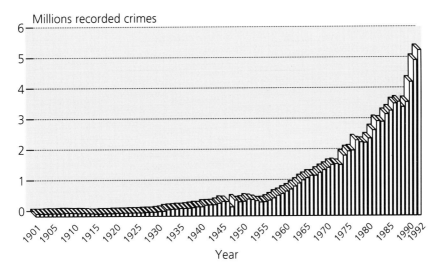

Source: Home Office Crime Statistics (including London)

2. The number of crimes cleared up in England and Wales in 1992 was 1.4 million, a rise of 23% since 1982. However, because of the increase in recorded crime, the proportion of crime solved by the police (the clear-up or detection rate) has declined from 37% in 1982 to 26% in 1992. Because the clear-up rate is the headline figure, police performance appears to have deteriorated. However, using crime statistics as a measure of police performance needs care. For example, a murder counts the same as the theft of a milk bottle. Even when the statistics are disaggregated into Home Office categories such as non-domestic burglary or fraud, these categories still contain crimes at opposite ends of a spectrum of seriousness. For example, 'burglary non-dwelling' could range from the theft of a spade from a garden shed to a million-pound seizure from a warehouse. It is therefore difficult to break down the crime figures into categories such as 'serious' or 'minor' even though this would be more logical from the perspective of the citizen, and more useful for the purpose of analysis.

---

1   *The number of crimes quoted throughout the report excludes offences of criminal damage of value £20 and under, unless stated otherwise.*

3. The level of crime *recorded* by the police – that is, reported incidents which fall within the Home Office's definition of crime – is the principal statistic. However, this underestimates the extent of crime; many crimes are not even reported to the police. People may not report a crime because they feel it is too trivial, because there is little the police can do about it or because of negative attitudes towards the police. On the other hand, attitudes and behaviour can change. The Home Office-sponsored British Crime Survey (BCS) seeks to measure the true extent of crime by surveying householders on their experiences of crime and determining whether they reported these to the police.

4. This survey[1] shows an increasing propensity by the public to report crimes to the police. Some 28% of crimes were reported in 1981, compared with 43% in 1991, implying an underlying increase in crime over this period significantly lower than the increase for comparable offences shown in recorded crime statistics. Reasons for this change of behaviour include the increasing extent of household and car insurance, greater publicity given to formerly 'hidden' crimes such as child abuse, increasing ease of access to telephones and positive encouragement by the police for the public to come forward and report crimes.

5. International comparisons help to set a context. But comparisons between recorded crime statistics from different countries need to be treated with caution because of variation in the methods used to classify or record crimes and register detections. The International Crime Survey, a telephone survey of personal experiences of crime in developed countries which sought to apply consistent definitions, shows the risk of crime, and in particular crimes of assault, still to be lower in England and Wales than in some other developed countries (Exhibit 2).

6. Property crimes, and in particular burglary and vehicle-related offences, have risen significantly since 1982 (Exhibit 3). Although robbery shows one of the highest percentage increases, the actual number of offences is relatively small compared with the other categories. Crimes against the person (violence, sexual assault and robbery) account for only about 5% of all recorded crime (Exhibit 4, page 6), although they contribute disproportionately to peoples' fear of crime.

THE CRIMINAL JUSTICE SYSTEM

7. One approach in analysing the crime problem is to identify four elements:

— the causes of crime;

— measures to reduce or prevent the commission of crime;

— investigation of crime and apprehension of offenders;

— prosecution of offenders and sentencing of those convicted.

Rising crime figures and falling clear-up rates often prompt criticism of the police. However, police work needs to be seen in the context of the whole system of criminal justice and society (Exhibit 5, page 6).

8. The police are not responsible for the causes of crime, the roots of which lie deep in society. Tackling the causes requires action on a broad front by both central and local government in fields

---

1   *Home Office Research and Planning Unit, Bulletin on the 1991 British Crime Survey, London, 1992.*

Exhibit 2
PERCENTAGE OF THE POPULATION WHO WERE VICTIMS OF CRIME IN 1991
Although the crime rate in England and Wales has been rising, citizens in some other developed
countries face a greater risk of being victims, especially of violent crime ...

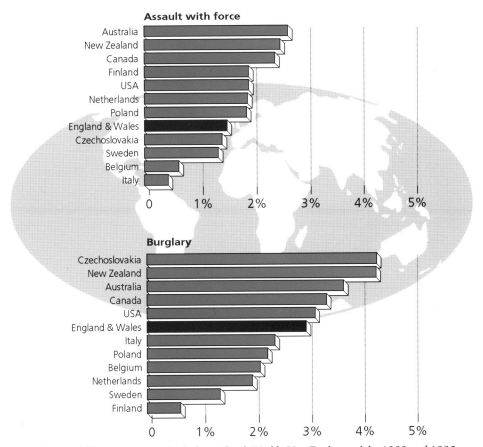

*Source: Criminal Victimisation in the Industrialised World: Key Findings of the 1989 and 1992
International Crime Surveys, J. Van Dijk and P. Mayhew, The Hague, Ministry of Justice,
1992*

Exhibit 3
INCREASES IN RECORDED CRIME 1982-1992, BY MAIN CATEGORIES
The crimes of robbery, criminal damage and theft from vehicles have shown the largest percentage
increases...

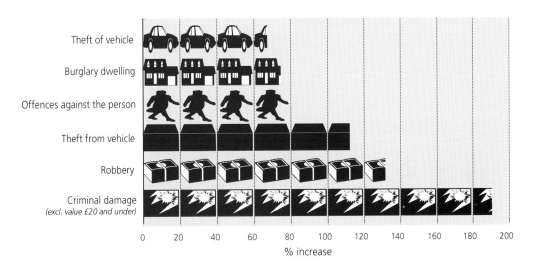

*Source: Criminal Statistics England & Wales, 1991, HMSO (figures include London); Home Office
Statistical Bulletin 9/93*

Exhibit 4

MIX OF CRIMES IN ENGLAND & WALES, 1992

Around 5% of recorded crimes are against the person; the vast majority – 94% – are against property ...

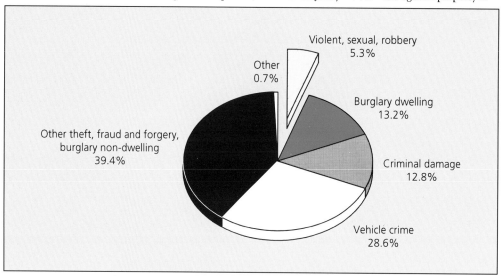

Source: Home Office Statistical Bulletin 9/93 (including London)

Exhibit 5

THE CRIMINAL JUSTICE SYSTEM IN CONTEXT

The police are only one agency influencing crime prevention and detection; many other agencies within and outside the criminal justice system play a role...

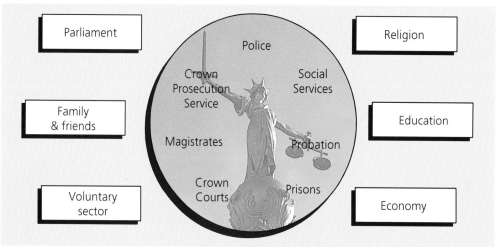

such as education, training, social services and probation. Criminality is not confined to a small minority, but is evident at some time in the lives of many. One disturbing finding from Home Office analysis of criminal records is that 33% of males born in a particular year had been convicted of at least one 'standard list' offence by the age of thirty, although many of these had only one conviction[1]. Socio-economic characteristics such as levels of deprivation may be important; and demographic factors such as the proportion of young people can also be significant, as almost 50% of detected crime is committed by persons under the age of 21 years.

---

1   *Home Office Statistical Bulletin 32/89.*

9. The police do play an important role in reducing and preventing crime, as one agency in a partnership that embraces government, business and individuals. But, for example, the police cannot be held responsible if cars are manufactured with poor security or if individual citizens do not, in the words of the 1993 White Paper on Police Reform, 'do all that can be reasonably expected of them to protect their own property'.

10. The third element, the investigation of crimes and the apprehension of offenders, is clearly a substantive responsibility of the police and is the focus of this report. But once the police have prepared case files, it is the independent Crown Prosecution Service which reviews the evidence and decides whether a prosecution should be brought. If a case does reach court, the police role is relatively limited; they provide protection to witnesses, in increasingly difficult circumstances, give evidence and make representations on matters such as bail. They do not decide upon verdicts, and officers often express frustration that persistent offenders are released after sentencing only to re-offend immediately.

11. The effectiveness of the police is thus dependent on other parts of the criminal justice system, which is designed to impose checks and balances upon unfettered executive action. This report makes reference to a number of demands and constraints, such as the need for typed summaries of interviews and disclosure of material collected during investigation, which consume police resources and impinge upon their effectiveness. It would be inappropriate, given that the study examined only the police, to draw conclusions about these matters, but they form part of the background against which police performance should be assessed.

POLICE PERFORMANCE

12. The police account for approximately two thirds of the total expenditure on the criminal justice system. Between 1982 and 1992 the number of police officers in England and Wales rose by 6% to 128,045; if civilian staff are included the total staff increase was 12%. Total capital and revenue spending on the police rose in real terms by 43% between 1982 and 1992, partly because of staffing increases but also due to the index-linking of police salaries. In the financial year 1992/93 total revenue expenditure on the police was £5.68 billion, around £110 per head of population.[1]

13. However, this rise in police resources has been outstripped by the increase in demand for police services – calls for assistance, traffic incidents as well as crime reports (Exhibit 6, overleaf). Recorded crimes per officer (uniformed and CID) rose from an average of 26 per officer in 1982 to 42 per officer in 1992. Despite this increase in workload, police officers have solved an increasing number of crimes each year; productivity, as measured by clear-ups per officer, has risen by around 16% over the decade. But because these productivity increases have been outpaced by the surge in recorded crime, the overall clear-up *rate* declined during the 1980s down to the current national level of 26%. Overall clear-up rates in individual provincial forces range from 53% to 17%.

---

1   *The relevant figures for provincial forces, i.e. excluding the City of London and the Metropolitan Police, are as follows: police officer strength rose by 5.6% to 99,033; total staff increase including civilians was 14.8%; total spending increased by 43.6%; expenditure in 1992/93 was £4.2 billion or £96 per head.*

Exhibit 6
CHANGES IN POLICE RESOURCES AND DEMAND FOR POLICE SERVICES 1982-1992
Each year the police dealt with more crimes, more calls for assistance and an increased volume of traffic;
staffing levels have not kept pace with these increases...

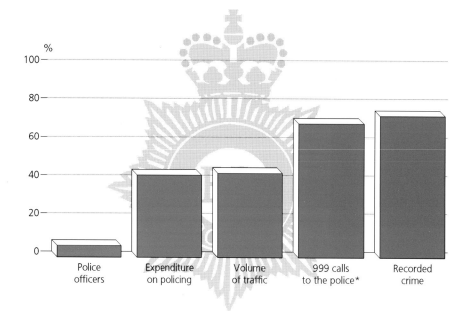

* 1981 - 1991 for 999 calls

*Source: Home Office Crime Statistics, CIPFA expenditure figures, ACPO 10-year survey,
Department of Transport figures on traffic volume, HMIC staffing figures*

14. The primary clear-up rate,[1] which is a more robust comparative indicator of police effectiveness than the overall clear-up rate, varies amongst provincial forces from 40% to 13%. Those forces with higher overall clear-up rates are not necessarily the most efficient. The wide variations in clear-up rates can be explained partly by variations in efficiency, partly by demographic factors and partly by workload, which ranges from a low workload of 36 officers (uniformed and CID) per 1,000 crimes in Dyfed-Powys to 15 in Nottinghamshire. Forces with fewer officers per 1,000 crimes tend to have lower clear-up rates, although there is also a considerable variation in performance amongst forces with similar workloads (Exhibit 7). These variations are largely due to differences in organisation, systems and productivity, rather than to factors such as the mix of crime.

15. At existing crime levels, if every provincial force matched the force with the highest clear-ups per officer within its family[2], the overall clear-up rate would rise to around 37%. However, if the improvement in productivity over the next decade is no greater than that achieved in the last, then, given current trends in crime figures and clear-ups, by 2002 the number of

---

1   *There are six classifications used to record clear-ups, divided into primary and secondary categories. The six methods of clear-up are (i) charge or summons (ii) caution (iii) no further action (where the offender is known but there are grounds for not pursuing a prosecution) (iv) taken into consideration – TIC – where the offence was previously recorded (v) TIC where the offence was not previously recorded and (vi) prison write-offs i.e. admissions to other offences secured from an offender already in custody. Categories (i) to (iv) are treated in this report as primary clear-ups.*

2   *The families of forces are defined in Police Paper No. 8.*

Exhibit 7

RELATIONSHIP BETWEEN PRIMARY CLEAR-UP RATE AND OFFICERS PER 1,000 CRIMES A YEAR

Forces with fewer officers per 1,000 crimes tend to have lower clear-up rates ...

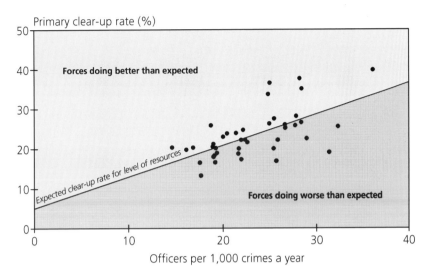

Note: *Correlation co-efficient:* $r = 0.62$. *This linear relationship should not be extrapolated much beyond the highest observed number of officers per 1,000 crimes because, theoretically, at some point there will be diminishing returns from increases in resources and ultimately a maximum clear-up rate will be attained.*

Source: *Audit Commission analysis of Home Office Crime Statistics and HMIC Matrix data for 1992 (excludes London forces)*

recorded crimes will exceed 9 million and the overall clear-up rate could drop to 18%. Society is thus in danger of losing the 'battle against crime'. Notwithstanding the responsibilities of other agencies to address themselves more effectively to the crime problem, police managers must make improvements. A starting point is a clear, objective analysis of the situation, which is the subject of the next chapter.

1. The Police Response to Crime

16. The current police approach to crime management has evolved over the last three decades, but neither nationally nor locally in most forces has there been an across-the-board review of its efficiency and effectiveness. This chapter examines the management arrangements and investigative practices to identify the scope for improvement.

AN INTEGRATED APPROACH?

17. Over the years all forces have taken initiatives to tackle crime. However, these have often not succeeded in galvanising the entire force – traditional departmentalism has been an impediment. Forces need a corporate management approach to exploit the best ideas and inspire the commitment of the entire force. Although the particular circumstances of mounting an effective police response to crime are unique, the underlying issues are amenable to standard management appraisal. Such an appraisal should address:

— the definition of the specific problems to be tackled;

— an order of priority for their resolution;

— the rational allocation of resources;

— a clear statement of roles and accountabilities;

— appropriate structures to deploy resources and meet objectives.

In considering how well the management of crime fares against this yardstick the starting point is to define core problems, or to ask 'what business are the police in?' This question has become increasingly difficult to answer.

DEFINING CORE PROBLEMS

18. In 1829 the first Commissioners of the Metropolitan Police, Rowan and Mayne, declared that:

> 'The principal object to be attained is the prevention of crime. To this great end every effort of the police is to be directed.'

The complexity of modern policing does not admit the luxury of such a simple mission statement. The boundaries of police activity have expanded to meet new demands and have shifted from a narrow enforcement perspective to a wider concept of public service. Some argue that to define the service's core role too precisely would constrain the flexibility required to police a constantly changing society. But when the increasing demands on the service lead to the police and public being unsure of roles and priorities, clarification becomes vital.

11

19. The Association of Chief Police Officers (ACPO) tried to resolve this problem by defining five 'key service areas', of which crime management is one (Exhibit 8). However, there is no indication of the relative level of resources that should be assigned to each area, and it is hard to envisage *any* police activity which could not be slotted into one of them. A lack of local solution is attracting central prescription; the need for clarity on policing priorities is recognised in the recent White Paper on Police Reform. This listed five main aims of the police service and signalled the government's intention to set key national objectives; it further declared that 'fighting crime and the protection of the public should be the top priority in police work '.

Exhibit 8
ACPO AND HOME OFFICE STATEMENTS OF KEY AREAS AND MAIN AIMS
ACPO has defined five key service areas, whilst the Home Office has set five main aims of policing ...

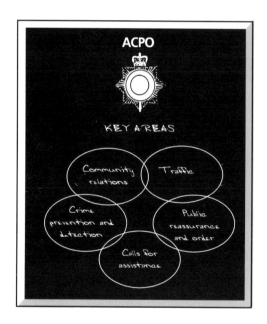

CRIME STRATEGY – SETTING PRIORITIES

20. In seeking priorities, the police have increasingly consulted the public and responded to their views. They have had to reconcile ever-increasing, often contradictory, expectations with a professional assessment of what is feasible and efficient. Thus the need to make an effective response to crime has to be balanced with putting more officers on street patrol. Other public services such as the NHS face a similar problem of demand exceeding resources; their response is to ration effort and concentrate upon the top priorities. Police forces face difficulties in attempting this, especially in relation to crime. The logic underpinning policing decisions may not be matched by the rationality of the public response. It is not realistic to expect the same degree of effort to be applied to the theft of a car as to a child murder, but when the police do try to make gradations of investigative effort explicit they are accused of decriminalising certain offences and increasing the fear of crime. Therefore they attempt to fulfil all of their responsibilities, however thinly. The police might justifiably argue that never in the history of police activity has so much been expected of them.

21. However, where chief officers or police authorities have not grasped this nettle of prioritisation, individual police officers – being pragmatic people – have made their own rationing decisions. Although it is done with the best of intentions, it is strategy by default, and could impair the delivery of a consistent service across the force. Moreover, the judgements about priorities made by police officers, based in large part on their professional experience, may differ from those of the average citizen. Some crimes of public concern, such as vandalism, have a low priority with most police officers.

CRIME STRATEGY – THE ROLE OF CRIME PREVENTION

22. In any statement of police aims, crime prevention is expressed as a high priority. The police have a long record of initiative in crime prevention, and during the last decade their approach has broadened to encompass not just personal and domestic security measures but also advice on 'designing out' crime on housing estates and in car parks. Encouraged by the Home Office, forces have engaged in partnership initiatives with local authorities and other agencies, such as the Safer Cities projects. These have shown impressive results, especially when supported with additional funding (Box A). However, police efforts are sometimes impaired by a lack of commitment from other partners to the multi-agency approach (Box B, overleaf). The Morgan Report's recommendation that crime prevention responsibilities be set within a statutory frame-work was not accepted by the government. Another impediment is the absence of an agreed duty of care by the public, in particular householders and car-owners.

Box A
CRIME PREVENTION IN ACTION

Merseyside Police used Urban Crime Fund money to install closed-circuit television cameras at the entrances to sheltered accommodation for the elderly which had been plagued by 'bogus official' burglaries, where thieves had talked themselves into homes by pretending to be council or utility company officials. In the twelve months prior to the installation there had been 51 burglaries, all investigated exhaustively by the police. In the year since the cameras were installed, only nine burglaries have occurred.

A joint police/local council project in inner city Leicester reduced burglaries by 62%, through improved domestic security.

The establishment of the Motor Education Project in Bradford has coincided with a reduction of 75% in the number of new autocrime offenders coming to police attention during the 18 months up to June 1993.

The introduction of closed-circuit TV cameras into Airdrie town centre, with public support, has had dramatic results. In the first twelve months of operation, recorded crimes dropped from 2,475 to 627, of which 447 (71%) were cleared up. Break-ins to commercial premises dropped from 263 to 15 and incidents of vandalism from 207 to 36. The reduced workload in incident response has allowed increased patrol in rural areas. The costs of installation and maintenance are met by the local business community.

Box B
WEAKNESSES IN THE MULTI-AGENCY APPROACH: A CASE STUDY

> A town centre shop was ram-raided seven times in less than a year, despite the installation of alarms and some expensive police surveillance work. Eventually, the insurers informed the manager that unless security shutters were installed, the shop's insurance cover would be withdrawn. An application was duly made to the local council, with the support of the police, for permission to install the shutters. Despite previous declarations supporting the fight against crime, the council turned down the application on the grounds that shutters would lower the tone of the shopping area. The business was forced to close.

23. Overall, however, the police emphasise the detection of crime rather than its prevention. In too many forces crime prevention is a relatively low-status, poorly resourced activity. Crime prevention officers (CPOs) are typically constables with an average age of 42 and 20 years' service; about three quarters have never worked in CID[1]. Whilst experience is important, such a profile is not indicative of a dynamic role accorded high status by senior management. The number of officers assigned specifically to crime prevention work is around 1% of police strength, compared to some 40% of effort put into investigation. The most senior officer managing crime prevention work is usually an inspector or chief inspector; it is managed not alongside investigation but rather alongside a disparate range of community liaison work. CPOs rarely work closely with detectives even when the function is nominally located in CID, and tend not to be involved in the analysis of crime patterns.

---

1   *Source: an Audit Commission questionnaire covering a range of issues related to crime management, which was completed by 85% of provincial forces.*

24. Detection is an immediate and visible measure of police success and it is what detectives are trained to accomplish; but the public would no doubt prefer a low crime rate to a high detection rate. Prevention and detection are often perceived as separate strands of activity when they should be inextricably linked; effective crime prevention enhances relationships with the community and should therefore help to create a climate for co-operation with the police on crime detection. Some forces are addressing this issue; Cumbria and Hertfordshire, for example, have greatly enhanced the status of CPOs, moving away from the 'bolts and bars' advice to burglary victims to more analytical work such as identifying crime 'hot spots', for example vulnerable car parks, and devising tactics to reduce the incidence of crime in these areas. The 'bolts and bars' advice is in fact more efficiently given by the officer who first attends the scene of the burglary.

ALLOCATING RESOURCES RATIONALLY

25. The fourth element of appraisal concerns the share of overall resources allocated to dealing with crime and mechanisms for its internal distribution. During the 1960s, benchmark figures for detective establishments emerged from the Home Office and Her Majesty's Inspectorate of Constabulary (HMIC). They continue to influence assessments of CID strength. Although the volume of crime has risen significantly, the relative size of CID within each force has remained fairly constant at around 15% of force strength, despite significant variations between forces in crime levels. A further 25% of police work involves crime response and investigation by uniformed officers, giving a total commitment to work generated by crime incidents of around 40% of resources, at an approximate cost of £2.3 billion for England and Wales (Exhibit 9). In many forces, CID attention is now directed towards fewer but more serious investigations, whilst uniformed officers deal with up to 80% of crime reports.

Exhibit 9
PERCENTAGE OF POLICE RESOURCES INVOLVED IN CRIME RESPONSE AND INVESTIGATION
Some 40% of total police effort is in responding to and investigating crime incidents ...

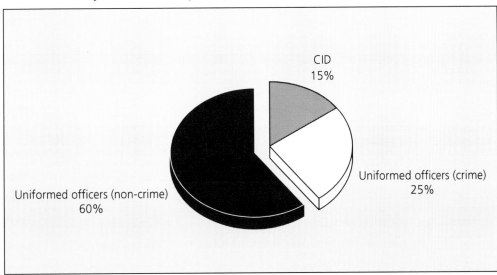

Source: estimate based upon activity analysis data supplied by a large metropolitan, a medium-size and a rural force

26. Another key issue is deployment i.e. the number of detectives assigned to each territorial unit of policing, the basic command unit (BCU). Forces often use fairly sophisticated formulae for the allocation of uniformed officer resources, but systematic assessments of the relative need for CID are less common. Decisions are often incremental adjustments to historically based benchmarks such as caseload per detective or overall crime levels, driven by a process of bidding for extra resources sometimes referred to as 'decibel planning'.

27. Forces suffer from a paucity of the information which would help make more informed assessments. For example, in most forces there is scant information about the time spent per investigation, as opposed to time spent upon a category of activity. The knowledge that one BCU dealt with 2,000 burglaries whilst its neighbour dealt with 2,000 assaults cannot in itself guide a resourcing decision which seeks to equalise workload per officer across the force, because the average length of time needed to deal with these crimes is not captured.

28. Force reviews have tended to avoid a root and branch review of the share of resources given to CID. One reason is that forces feel constrained by HMIC benchmarks. However, without a clear rationale, there is a risk that function follows form, rather than determining it. Instead of using a clear statement of the detective's role to determine how many are needed, some police managers take CID establishment as given and ensure that commensurate amounts of work flow into it regardless of whether this work merits the attention of experienced detectives. What is needed is a clear definition of the role of CID.

THE ROLE OF CID

29. The original remit of CID was clear. Individual detective officers began operating in 1842, but a terrorist bombing in London in 1867 prompted the establishment of a specialist investigation department. Its brief included the tracking of local criminals, the use of observation to deter and detect crime, and the cultivation of paid informants. The work necessitated the adoption of plain clothes and the methods were viewed by the public with some suspicion as a form of espionage. The growth of CID over the next half century was slow but steady. By the time of the Cornish Report in 1963 all 122 police forces had a CID, staffed on the basis of approximately 150 cases per officer per year, with detectives tackling all crime work; uniformed officers might respond to a crime incident but all investigations were conducted by detectives.

30. But the rapid growth in the volume of crime, combined with a static share of resources in CID, has reduced the clarity of its role. Clearly, the investigation of all crime is no longer a specialist role, because the bulk of that work is undertaken by uniformed officers, who have relatively little training in investigative techniques and in some cases little interest in acquiring them (Exhibit 10). However, their contribution to detection is significant; analysis by the Commission of a sample of detected, serious crimes – burglary, robbery and sexual assault – revealed that uniformed officer activities, such as enquiries at the scene and 'stop and search' procedures, were the principal source of detection in 27% of cases.

31. Because no force can assign all crime work solely to detectives, just over half of forces designate serious crime, which is likely to be more complex and arouse greater public concern, as the threshold to determine whether or not CID become involved. A threshold implies that serious crimes can be investigated adequately only by a detective. However, there is no consensus about

what constitutes a serious crime. Some crimes such as murder, rape and armed robbery would be classified as serious by all police forces, as well as the public, but there are some 'grey areas'.

Exhibit 10
THE ORGANISATIONAL RESPONSE TO CRIME IN ONE FORCE
Different types of crime are dealt with by different branches of the police; typically, less than a quarter of crimes are investigated by detectives ...

Category of crime	Typical response	% crimes
Minor crime	Filed after recording	24%
Less serious crime e.g. theft from vehicle	Uniformed constable at BCU investigates	53%
Serious crime e.g. burglary	Detective constable at BCU investigates	20%
Very serious crime e.g. rape, murder	HQ/Force-wide squad or specialist team	3%
Major crime crossing force boundary	Refer to Regional Crime Squad	<0.1%

Source: Audit Commission analysis of data provided by a study force

What crimes do CID investigate?

32. The categories of crime investigated by CID differ from force to force (Exhibit 11). This raises questions about definitions of detectives as specialists whose experience and expertise are vital elements of effective investigation. If on one day or in one force a crime merits the attention

Exhibit 11
CRIMES INVESTIGATED BY CID IN STUDY FORCES
Crimes investigated by detectives in one force may be dealt with in another force by uniformed officers ...

Crime	Forces				
	A	B	C	D	E
Murder / serious assault	✔	✔	✔	✔	✔
Sexual assault	✔	✔	✔	✔	✔
Robbery	✔	✔	✔	✔	✔
Deception	✔	✔	✔	✔	✔
Drugs offence	✘	✘	✔	✔	✘
Burglary dwelling	S	✔	✔	✔	✔
Burglary non-dwelling	✘	✘	✔	✔	✘
High-value other theft	✘	✘	✘	✔	✔
Theft of motor vehicle	✘	✘	✘	✔	✘
Minor assault	✘	✘	✘	✔	✘
Theft from motor vehicle	✘	✘	✘	✘	✘
Other theft	✘	✘	✘	✘	✘

✔ - Yes   ✘ - No   S - Sometimes

Source: Audit Commission analysis

of a detective, but an identical case can be handled on another day or in another force by a relatively inexperienced PC, then the argument for a role definition as a specialist invites challenge.

33. Even where forces have categorised crimes and defined when and why cases are assigned to detectives, day to day practice may depart from theory. The fact that detectives investigate some less serious crimes is not in itself evidence of poor practice – for example, such a crime may have been committed by a serious criminal being targeted by CID. But it can be construed as poor practice if there is a lack of awareness of or rationale for this pattern of activity. In one of the study forces more than half of CID investigative activity was related to less serious offences which, according to the force's own procedures, should have been allocated to beat officers (Exhibit 12).

Exhibit 12
THE WORKLOAD OF DETECTIVE CONSTABLES IN ONE FORCE
Serious crime as defined by the force was intended to comprise most of a detective's time but in practice comprises less than half the time spent on investigation...

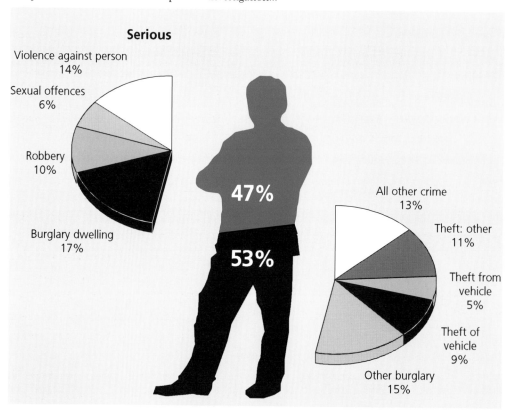

Source: Audit Commission analysis of data from one study force

34. There are five main reasons why detectives are drawn into involvement in relatively minor crime matters:

— *the shift patterns of uniformed officers*: it is unclear whether CID is justified as a large corps of skilled officers needed to tackle serious investigations, or more prosaically because crime work is logistically difficult to manage within the present shift systems worked by uniformed officers. Although senior officers point to the former reason as the theoretical rationale for CID, in practice the latter seems as important. A PC may begin work on a case but then, on

18

the Ottawa shift system, go on night shift followed by five or six days leave. If the investigation thus needs to be re-assigned, prevailing shift culture may lead to a referral to CID rather than to an incoming shift;

— *uniformed competence:* there is evidence of poor performance by uniformed officers on crime investigation attributable to inadequate training or experience (a high proportion of PCs on patrol are probationers); a fire-fighting style of deployment, rushing from one incident to another; flaws in supervision; and an attitude that 'crime is not my responsibility, it's CID work'. Even where the PC's initial investigation is competent there is a pattern in many forces of handing the part-completed crime file to CID for completion;

— *the Police and Criminal Evidence Act 1984 (PACE) requirements:* a person arrested during the night may not be fit to be interviewed, or may request a solicitor who cannot attend immediately. PACE imposes a strict timetable for detention, and early shift detectives may be required to interview prisoners 'before the clock runs out'. This involves them, often for a whole morning, in interviews with people arrested by officers who have since gone off duty, for offences outside the normal purview of CID;

— *case allocation:* many forces use a system of assessment or screening to allocate cases to either uniformed officers or CID. If the criteria are not adhered to or are administered inefficiently, detectives may be assigned cases which are neither serious nor form part of a linked series of crimes;

— *clear-up targets:* there is constant pressure to improve the clear-up rate and CID may be tempted to achieve this relatively quickly by a 'blitz' upon less serious crime.

STRUCTURE AND ACCOUNTABILITIES FOR CRIME MANAGEMENT

35. Until recently the typical force structure had three operational tiers – headquarters, divisions and sub-divisions. Detectives working in a sub-division had a dual accountability, to the uniformed commander of their sub-division and to senior detectives. Approximately three quarters of forces have now removed the divisional tier, to shorten lines of communication and delegate responsibility to 'front-line' managers. The responsibility for operational matters which is now delegated to BCU commanders, typically of superintendent rank, marks a radical change and has particular implications for crime management – CID is no longer a department in the conventional sense. Although the demarcation between CID and uniformed officers has been eroded in recent years, it has not completely disappeared. Local detectives are now accountable, in theory, only to the uniformed BCU commander, but in practice the position is less clear-cut.

36. In some force HQs senior detective officers are referred to as 'CID command'; this sends out a mixed message given that they no longer command the bulk of detective resources. Senior detectives often see their role as detectives first and managers second, attaching considerable importance to heading up major investigations, even though they rarely discharge this role – 62% of CID heads have not done so within their own force within the last year. They do, however, perform a key role in developing force-wide crime strategies and in relation to specialist investigation squads.

37. In some forces changes are still bedding down and there are lessons to be learned from those forces which restructured some time ago. The strategic role of headquarters CID in, for

example, determining resource needs and monitoring performance needs clarification at an early stage. However, key tasks related to this strategic role, such as policy analysis and performance review, are often carried out in departments other than CID. Thus instead of *owning* these tasks, CID managers are obliged to engage in departmental struggles for influence around them, including a degree of empire-building over the allocation of resources.

Specialist squads

38. There are two principal reasons why forces establish specialist squads. One is that some crimes, such as major frauds, require specialist expertise and equipment and a centralised squad offers economies of scale. The other reason is that, although the bulk of crimes are local in nature, some criminals operate across the whole force area and beyond, and the response to them must be closely co-ordinated and directed from HQ. The study forces varied in their configuration of squads (Exhibit 13) and their relative size, ranging from 12% of crime staff up to 40%. There is also considerable variation across all forces in the criteria for deployment, tenure policies and the measures used to gauge effectiveness.

Exhibit 13
CONFIGURATION OF SQUADS IN FIVE STUDY FORCES
All study forces have a fraud squad, but the pattern of other squad establishment varies ...

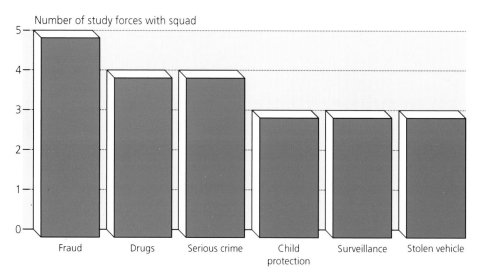

Source: information from study forces

39. Most squads – around 83% – have terms of reference setting out the criteria for their acceptance of a case. However, such criteria do not prevent ambiguity or disputes arising. A common complaint, expressed in one third of interviews conducted by the study team, was that the squads were not providing an adequate service to BCUs but were generating their own work. This reflects ambiguity or tension about the extent to which squads should operate autonomously from, or in direct support of, BCUs; ACPO has recently issued guidelines which stress the importance of effective supervision of squads and corporate accountability[1].

---

1   *Report of Sub Group Considering the Use of Specialist Squads, ACPO Crime Committee.*

40. Two thirds of forces have tenure policies laying down the maximum period for which an officer can be attached to a squad. These vary from force to force and are not always based upon a rational assessment of the costs and benefits of differing tenure periods i.e. taking account of the varying learning curves for specialist work. Collaboration between one force and the Audit Commission on such an assessment suggested that the minimum tenure period for fraud squad officers should be four years to justify the investment in training and learning the job, yet in some forces the tenure period applying to fraud duties is three years. More crucially, some forces lack the means to assess the relative effectiveness of the squad approach. If squads are not tasked to achieve results over and above those which could be achieved if the work remained at BCU level, then there must be a question mark over their raison d'être. Merseyside is addressing this problem by developing performance indicators for its serious crime squad.

Crime management at the BCU level

41. An immediate complication of restructuring is that almost two thirds of BCU commanders do not have CID experience. Some in this situation are less inclined to take full responsibility for managing detectives and thus weaken the coherence of BCU operations. They may also lack credibility with their detectives, who seek ways of circumventing commanders in organising their activities. The senior-ranking detectives in the BCUs, usually detective inspectors but chief inspectors in some larger BCUs, still look over their shoulders to the CID hierarchy, to whom daily briefings are given and who may be responsible for part of their annual appraisal.

42. There is an ambiguity about the role of the senior detective in the BCU (Exhibit 14). Although he or she is often titled 'crime manager', it is often unclear whether this officer is expected to manage the response to *all* crime occurring within the BCU patch, or only those

Exhibit 14
TYPICAL MANAGEMENT STRUCTURE OF A BASIC COMMAND UNIT
The rigid demarcation between CID and uniformed officers has eroded over time, but in practice some fragmentation persists...

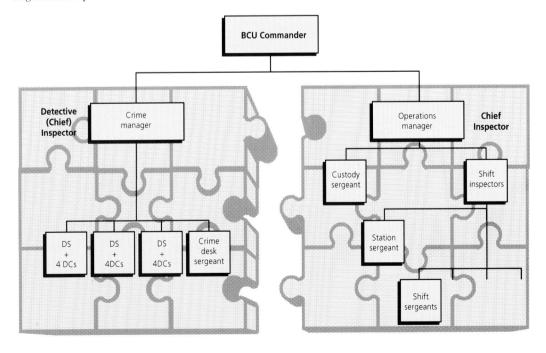

crimes falling within the CID remit. If it is the latter, then there is potential incoherence in the way that the BCU manages crime problems as a whole. There is also a danger that BCU commanders may adopt too parochial a view of crime. If parochialism predominates, the force risks losing control of an important swathe of crime which transcends BCU boundaries. Delegating more responsibilities to BCU commanders has significant benefits but should not allow corporate issues to become marginalised.

43. There is thus room for improvement in adopting a more integrated approach to crime work. Priorities could be more explicit, with a greater profile given to crime prevention. The role of detective, and the specific skills needed to discharge that role, require clearer definition. The basis of resource allocation in some forces is obscure and there remains a blurring of accountability, although these problems are to some degree ones of new structures bedding down.

MAKING THE MOST EFFECTIVE USE OF RESOURCES

44. The police are unlikely to experience in the 1990s the increases in staffing levels which were a feature of the 1980s. It is therefore incumbent upon police managers to secure maximum benefit from available resources by addressing inefficiency in the management and deployment of officers.

DUPLICATION OF EFFORT IN THE FIRST RESPONSE

45. There is scope for improvement in the deployment of officers responding to the report of a crime. In the case of burglary dwelling investigations, the typical approach is to send the 'first available officer', a uniformed constable, to the scene within ten to fifteen minutes of the report (Exhibit 15). The officer records basic details of the incident but rarely has the time, or in some

Exhibit 15
THE TYPICAL RESPONSE TO A REPORT OF A BURGLARY
A typical response to a report of a burglary entails visits by three or four officers...

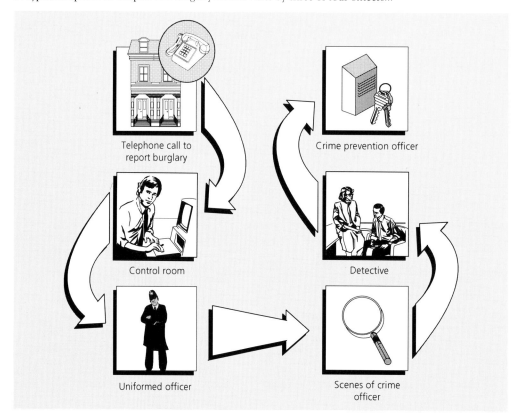

Telephone call to report burglary

Crime prevention officer

Control room

Detective

Uniformed officer

Scenes of crime officer

cases the expertise, to conduct an investigation. The officer knows that the 'real' investigation will be undertaken by a detective and the scenes of crime officer; in 75% of burglary incidents sampled during the Commission's fieldwork a detective visited the burglary scene. Detectives typically arrive within several hours of the PC, usually without an appointment. The victim repeats details of the crime, and may do so again if the local beat officer or crime prevention officer also calls. Where two or more officers visit at different times they do not always speak to each other about the case, especially if the detective is based at a different station from the PC.

46. Whilst acknowledging the potential for duplication of effort, some forces believe that multiple visits reflect public expectations and thus deliver a higher quality of service than attendance by just one officer. The Commission sought to test this assumption by undertaking a survey[1] of burglary victims, the results of which suggest that there is over-provision of service in some forces (Exhibit 16). For example, less than half the victims expected the police to treat the crime as an emergency, and thus grade it as requiring 'immediate response'. Only 21% expected to see a detective.

Exhibit 16
EXPECTATIONS OF BURGLARY VICTIMS AND THE POLICE RESPONSE
The mismatch between the expectations of burglary victims and the typical police response means that in some forces there is an over-provision of service ...

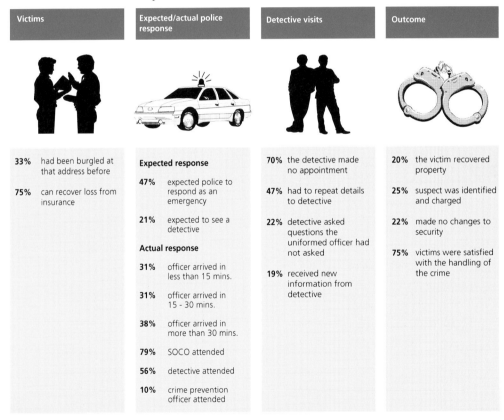

Victims	Expected/actual police response	Detective visits	Outcome
33% had been burgled at that address before	**Expected response**	**70%** the detective made no appointment	**20%** the victim recovered property
75% can recover loss from insurance	**47%** expected police to respond as an emergency	**47%** had to repeat details to detective	**25%** suspect was identified and charged
	21% expected to see a detective	**22%** detective asked questions the uniformed officer had not asked	**22%** made no changes to security
	Actual response		**75%** victims were satisfied with the handling of the crime
	31% officer arrived in less than 15 mins.	**19%** received new information from detective	
	31% officer arrived in 15 - 30 mins.		
	38% officer arrived in more than 30 mins.		
	79% SOCO attended		
	56% detective attended		
	10% crime prevention officer attended		

Source: Audit Commission survey of victims of burglary

---

1   *The Audit Commission appointed ICM to interview in their homes a sample of 230 victims of burglary and vehicle-related crime. The victims were drawn from four force areas and answered questions about the police response to the crime in relation to their expectations.*

47. There is often little added value derived from the detective's visit. One force analysed a sample of crime reports and found that in only around 3% of cases had the visit to the scene by detectives elicited valuable additional information. In the Commission's survey of victims only one in four victims reported that detectives undertook activities *not* carried out by the PC, such as interviewing neighbours. The crime reports sampled in the study forces indicated that activities carried out at the scene are often not recorded in detail, for example identifying who has been spoken to other than the victim. Too often, CID attend a burglary because of the poor quality – i.e. lack of detail, inconsistency or inadequacy – of crime reports completed by uniformed officers.

48. There are good reasons why detectives should attend at least some burglary scenes. Some offer valuable evidence-gathering opportunities – for example, where there has been contact between the burglar and the victim or witness. In other circumstances a victim may express a firm preference for a detective visit. Detective visits also provide feedback on the quality of the uniformed response, both in terms of the work that has or has not been carried out and the accuracy of its reporting. But without such clear and targeted purpose to the detectives' visits, particularly when they are routinely following a visit by a uniformed officer, forces will not utilise their CID resource efficiently. Also, they may not be making anticipated gains in consumer satisfaction. In the Commission's survey 47% of victims had to repeat details to the detective and only 19% were given new information by the detective.

ADEQUATE EQUIPMENT

49. One source of frustration for police managers charged with making the most efficient use of resources is that they are sometimes forced, because of inflexibility in the force's budget arrangements or a shortage of capital funds, into labour-intensive solutions to problems. For example, a major constraint in many forces is lack of cars – the 'traditional' practice of detectives working in pairs outside the CID office is often ascribed simply to the fact that they have to share a car. The Commission suggested[1] a benchmark ratio of about one car for every three CID officers; typically the ratio is one car for six detectives. Only 8% of detectives in BCUs have access to encrypted radios, providing secure communication which cannot be intercepted. Even in specialist squads, much of whose activity is covert and aimed at surveillance-conscious criminals, the percentage is only 58%. Information technology is often in short supply: in some forces up to thirty officers have to share one computer terminal and around 20% of forces do not have permanent major enquiry rooms fully equipped with the relevant computer and other technology.

MANAGEMENT OF INVESTIGATIONS

50. Investigations of major crimes such as murder or serial rape are now almost always supported by a customised software package (HOLMES, or Home Office Large Major Enquiry System). This information storage and retrieval system enables officers to index and interrogate large databases of enquiry evidence. Detection rates for major enquiries are high: for example, one of the study forces investigated 34 major incidents in 1991 and secured a 76% detection rate for the crimes concerned. Because of their complexity, such investigations tend to be long-running

---

1   *This benchmark figure was recommended in Police Paper No. 3 on vehicle fleet management, published by the Commission in 1989. Fewer cars will be needed in dense urban areas.*

and involve a heavy commitment of resources – typically up to 70 officers for the first few weeks and 30 officers subsequently if the crime is not solved quickly. Even a small degree of inefficient resourcing, such as failing to scale down the enquiry at the appropriate point, leads to a heavy abstraction from BCU investigations. Most, though not all, forces undertake formal reviews of undetected enquiries at specified intervals to monitor progress and the use of resources.

51. Fortunately, the majority of crimes do not require the HOLMES response; the investigative commitment can vary from this very intensive level down to just a few hours (Box C, overleaf). Some forces are, however, considering whether it is feasible to apply a scaled-down version of the approach used in major crime investigations to attack high-volume crime. For example, the software package can be adapted for smaller-scale enquiries to ease the management of data and provide the investigating officer with information about different lines of enquiry. Another characteristic is that in major enquiries the quality of officers' work is closely scrutinised, with the senior investigating officer adopting a very directive role. A strong team culture is also cited as a critical success factor, though this needs to be linked to close supervision.

SUPERVISION AND TEAMWORK

52. The major incident approach contrasts sharply with BCU-level investigations. In the latter, allocation of work is almost always to an individual officer rather than to a team. This can pose problems. Firstly, allocation may be made routinely on the basis of availability rather than expertise. Secondly, if crime pattern analysis or a similar technique has not identified linkages in offences, several detectives may unknowingly be working on crimes committed by the same individual. Thirdly, when the investigating officer is absent the case is rarely picked up by another officer unless the absence is prolonged. This may lead to a poor level of communication with victims or a degree of discontinuity in the investigation.

53. Most CID offices no longer have an office manager and the detective sergeant (DS) occupies this pivotal role. More crucially, the DS should supervise the work of the detective

Box C
POLICE RESPONSES TO THREE TYPES OF CRIME

(i) DOMESTIC BURGLARY

Hi-fi equipment worth £800 was stolen from a house; a uniformed constable attended the scene within 30 minutes and recorded the basic details of the crime. The case was then assigned to a detective constable who visited the house later that morning and made further enquiries, including interviewing neighbours. The victim was unable to provide serial numbers of the stolen items and there were no witnesses to the break-in. The following day a scenes of crime officer (SOCO) examined the house for fingerprints or other forensic evidence – none was found. Over the next week or so the detective liaised with the local intelligence officer and spoke to known informants. After nine days all leads had been exhausted and the file was closed.

Total officer time	:	5 hours
Investigation open	:	9 days
Status	:	undetected

(ii) 'STRANGER' RAPE

A female cyclist was attacked and raped by a man unknown to her. A detective inspector was appointed as the senior investigating officer, with a DS and three DCs to assist enquiries and a specially trained uniformed WPC to interview the victim. A SOCO examined the scene of the attack and the victim's clothing. The victim was able to give a description of her attacker and an artist's impression was widely publicised. A member of the public recognised this and named a possible suspect. The person was arrested, interviewed by detectives, and made a full confession. Corroborating evidence was provided by the forensic science laboratory from blood-stained clothing found at the house of the suspect's associate. The police charged the person with rape.

Total officer time	:	380 hours
Investigation open	:	8 days
Status	:	detected

(iii) MURDER

The victim was chased by a group of youths and struck by a brick thrown by one of them, dying from the injury. The police set up a major incident room and a detective superintendent took charge of the investigation. A large team of officers, up to 47 at the height of the enquiry, made enquiries and traced witnesses. The team comprised detectives, PCs and officers specially trained to undertake door-to-door enquiries. On the evidence of witnesses they traced, the team made several arrests and were then able to identify the youth who had thrown the brick.

Total officer time	:	1,350 hours
Investigation open	:	26 days
Status	:	detected

Source: case files

constables (DCs) reporting to him or her. The organisational culture, small team size and the pressured working environment disincline DSs to a formal style of supervision, which would set them apart from their teams. All of the DSs interviewed during the fieldwork for the study characterised their style of supervision as informal. This style is not in itself problematic and it reflects the fact that detectives apply themselves to their work with a very high degree of professionalism and commitment, often working many hours of unpaid overtime. However, certain features of CID work which flow from this approach merit reconsideration.

54. Detective constables may receive little or no guidance or direction about the nature and extent of enquiries to pursue, nor an indication of expected duration. This is not universal; Thames Valley recently addressed this point by introducing action plans which are given to detectives at the outset of the investigation. Frequently, progress reporting is *ad hoc*, and exception-based rather than systematic, which means that the DS may not be fully apprised of the stage that enquiries have reached. Added to this, the pressure upon detectives to 'get a result' causes some officers to hang on to files for too long after initial enquiries are exhausted, hoping for a breakthrough rather than accepting defeat. In a survey undertaken by the Commission of detected burglaries, robberies and sexual assaults, 75% of burglary detections occurred within ten days, 75% of sexual assaults within five days and 56% of robbery detections within five days.

55. Attempts to exercise more effective supervision may be impaired by:

— a workload which leaves little or no time for effective supervision: the DSs are in reality senior investigators, carrying a significant caseload and able to spend only a fraction of their time on direct supervision;

— a general absence of management information systems to record case allocation, monitor individual and team caseloads and track the progress of investigations (elapsed time, key stages, outcomes etc.);

— a system in which officers are promoted because of their technical skills as detectives rather than their supervisory potential and then receive little specific training in supervisory skills.

56. Supervision effort is directed at the product, the prosecution file or the undetected case file, and rarely at the process of investigation. Not surprisingly some errors occur – these are attributed to human factors rather than defects in supervisory procedures. DSs rarely accompany detectives on their enquiries or sit in on interviews – on fewer than 1% of occasions in one force which examined this point – although this is often the only satisfactory means of gauging the quality and quantity of work undertaken. Dip-sampling, whereby senior detectives listen in to a sample of interview tapes, is common practice although the emphasis is sometimes on compliance with PACE rather than the quality of the interrogation. However, it is often *ad hoc* and assessments of interviews are not co-ordinated to identify appropriate remedial action. Dyfed-Powys has tackled this by introducing a single-sheet interview appraisal form which evaluates technical points such as: establishment of the legal points; the style and manner of questioning (aggressive, searching etc.); and the quality of the interview summary.

Management of abstractions

57. Another issue which affects the efficient use of resources is the level of abstraction, i.e. the time that an officer is not available for normal duty, which can reach levels of 40% to 50%

in CID offices. The causes are various, with training, sickness, attendance at court and the attachment of detectives to major enquiry teams being the principal ones. Abstraction imposes a burden upon the detectives left in the office in dealing with an already heavy workload. Without computerised personnel information systems abstraction levels are hard to monitor, but they need to be kept under continuous review to mitigate the impact on crime investigation. Some factors are outside police control; West Midlands Police conducted a recent survey and found that only 20% of officers' time attending court is spent in giving evidence – the rest is waiting time. Activity analysis in other forces found even lower percentages. The Accounts Commission conducted a study in Scotland and similarly found that only 18% of officers attending court were called to the witness box[1].

BURDENSOME ADMINISTRATION

58. Some detectives feel that administrative tasks are a form of abstraction. Although the nature of police work inevitably generates such tasks, there is increasing concern about the extent of the 'paper chase' (Exhibit 17). Detectives complain that being tied to their desks by paperwork prevents them from getting on with their 'real' job of investigation and impairs a proactive approach. The task most commonly identified as absorbing productive time is the preparation of typed summaries of audio-taped interviews. Detectives cited estimates that this took up 20-30% of their time. In fact, activity analysis in three forces found that the preparation of tape summaries accounts for nearer 3%-6% of detective constables' time. The time commitment to other administrative tasks, notably file preparation, varies more widely (Table 1).

Table 1
PERCENTAGE OF DCs' TIME SPENT ON TAPE SUMMARIES AND FILE PREPARATION

% of DCs' time spent on:	Metropolitan force	Urban/rural force	Urban/rural force	Rural force
Tape summaries	3.0%	3.0%	5.1%	5.5%
File preparation	4.1%	9.6%	12.8%	20.4%
Total	7.1%	12.6%	17.9%	25.9%

Source: Audit Commission analysis of data supplied by four forces piloting activity analysis

59. Differences in file preparation time may be explained by differing degrees of accessibility to administrative support units (ASUs). Whilst ASUs' roles and structures vary from force to force, the common rationale is to streamline procedures and relieve officers of some paperwork. Although the burden upon operational officers has been generally alleviated, the impact of ASUs on detective work has not been as beneficial as originally anticipated, and they are seen increasingly as servicing the Crown Prosecution Service (CPS) rather than the force. Of those detectives interviewed, almost 60% described ASUs as advantageous, but some expressed concern about loss of 'ownership' once the file is passed to the ASU, and queried whether ASUs are competent to deal with more complex cases.

---

1   *Police Waiting Time at Court, the Accounts Commission for Scotland, 1992.*

Exhibit 17

THE PAPER CHASE

An arrest for even a relatively minor offence can entail a substantial degree of paperwork, with considerable duplication of information in the various forms ...

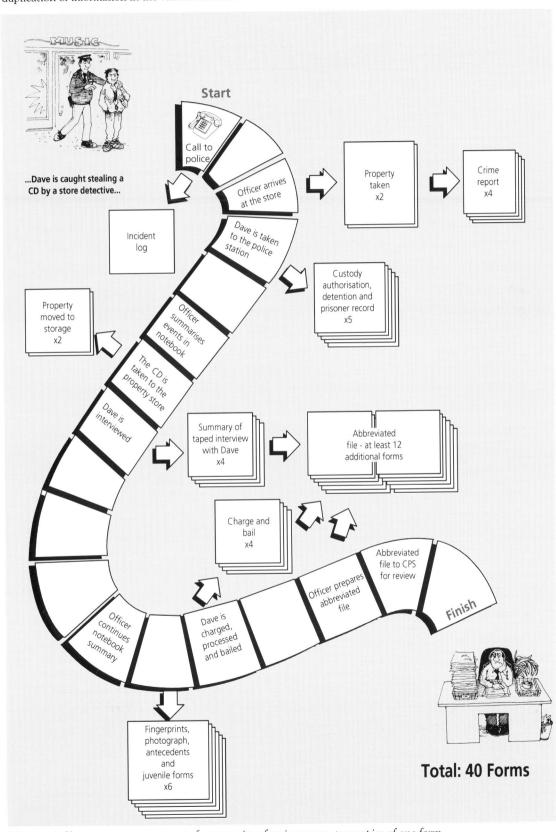

...Dave is caught stealing a CD by a store detective...

Start

Call to police

Officer arrives at the store

Property taken x2

Crime report x4

Incident log

Dave is taken to the police station

Custody authorisation, detention and prisoner record x5

Property moved to storage x2

Officer summarises events in notebook

The CD is taken to the property store

Dave is interviewed

Summary of taped interview with Dave x4

Abbreviated file - at least 12 additional forms

Charge and bail x4

Abbreviated file to CPS for review

Officer prepares abbreviated file

Finish

Officer continues notebook summary

Dave is charged, processed and bailed

Fingerprints, photograph, antecedents and juvenile forms x6

Total: 40 Forms

Note: 'x2' etc. means two separate forms or, in a few instances, two copies of one form.

Source: Audit Commission fieldwork and the Pre-Trial Issues Manual of Guidance

60. The introduction in October 1992 of Pre-Trial Issues (PTI) – a standardised national format for files which also sets time limits for submission to the CPS – has increased the workload of officers in 85% of forces, according to responses to the Commission's questionnaire. Officers interviewed generally welcomed the clarity and consistency introduced by PTI, but were concerned that the additional work involved had been underestimated. For example, PTI requires that a full file is prepared for all cases of assault even where the defendant has entered a guilty plea; formerly only a shorter or 'abbreviated' file would have been required. Rather than the original estimate of 40% of cases requiring full files, such files are being prepared in 60% of cases. Some 43% of detectives state that they are now more likely to complete their own files rather than send them to ASUs and risk being criticised for failing to meet the new deadlines for submission. Another recent development which has added to the administrative burden is the extension of the requirements governing disclosure of unused material to the defence. In one force visited during the study, monitoring of disclosure requirements absorbed the full-time equivalent of 23 officers during a sample week; this equates to 1% of force strength.

PERFORMANCE MANAGEMENT SYSTEMS

61. Many of the weaknesses in resource use outlined above reflect the inadequacy of performance management systems. Organisations need comprehensive systems for monitoring performance, to assess whether strategies are having the desired effect and to ensure efficient use of resources. Police forces generally do not have such systems in place in respect of crime work; although there is an abundance of statistics, robust performance indicators are in short supply. Historically, the most widely used indicator is the simple clear-up rate, which has flaws as a performance measure and is not accepted by detectives as a valid gauge of their effectiveness (Box D). However, there is no consensus about what constitutes a more robust measure; 42% of DSs interviewed offered no alternative but stressed that both the quality of work and the degree of effort injected should be reflected in performance measures for CID.

62. Many forces are striving to establish performance management frameworks within which the efforts and achievements of BCUs and individual officers can be evaluated. Good progress has been made recently; Kent, for example, has developed a comprehensive package of indicators and deployment data, in readable format, which is provided monthly to BCU commanders. Activity analysis, the record of how individual officers spend their time using a standard approach to classifying incidents and activities, will be increasingly valuable in improving the information basis for performance management. The importance of providing timely and relevant information to managers is generally recognised, but many forces are hampered by:

— restricted availability of information technology to speed up the processing and analysis of raw data;

— lack of clarity about what management information will best assist decision-making at BCU level on, for example, outputs and deployment, or the relative costs of different activities;

— the weight of other demands for information;

— an absence of clear targets against which performance can be measured, partly reflecting caution or mistrust that performance indicators will skew activities towards what is measurable rather than what is desired.

There are four major reasons why these statistics must be interpreted with care:

(i) **The volume of crime is not directly a measure of police performance**, rather one of demand for police services. Effective policing has some deterrent impact upon crime levels but other factors also come into play, for example: the number of additional offences added to the statute book each year; the rise in drug abuse, which is partly financed from criminal activities; and an increased propensity on the part of the public to report crime to the police.

(ii) **Aggregated crime statistics give equal weighting to each crime irrespective of seriousness**. For example, one murder counts the same as criminal damage to a bus shelter. Disaggregating into Home Office categories aids analysis but these categories still contain crimes at opposite ends of the spectrum in terms of seriousness: thus 'burglary other' encompasses a million-pound warehouse theft and theft from a garden shed. There is no standard classification of 'serious' crime.

(iii) **The definition of detection requires careful interpretation.** Many people assume that a crime is solved only when a person is either cautioned for or convicted of an offence, whereas a charge will count as a clear-up even if it is later rejected by the Crown Prosecution Service or the person found not guilty at court. Typically, about 90% of charges result in a conviction at court. Against this potential over-statement of the success rate must be set the fact that the CPS may not present in court all of the offences for which the police have some evidence of commission.

(iv) **Crimes vary greatly in their ease of detection**. Most studies show that the principal feature in clearing up crime is the availability of a witness who can identify the offender. Although the processing of such cases may be complex and time-consuming, it is a considerably greater challenge to investigate cases where the offender is initially unknown.

63. One element of performance management that needs more use in many forces is outcome analysis, the methodical assessment of the reasons for the success or failure of an investigation. A review of a major, HOLMES-based investigation where the senior investigator has the benefit of a computerised information base, and a log of decisions about lines of enquiry pursued or not pursued, is feasible. But for many investigations at BCU level, detectives have few records to refer to and often rely only upon personal experience. The police service, in the words of one officer interviewed, may need to develop a more robust 'learning culture'.

64. In summary, the police try hard to direct resources efficiently and monitor resource deployment – the recent introduction of activity analysis is testament to this. But, as in every organisation, there exists scope for improvement. There are four areas where system weaknesses impair the effort to make the best use of resources:

— the initial response to crime reports involves duplication of effort, largely because it is too driven by rapid incident response – akin to trying to manage a hospital through the Accident and Emergency Department;

— investigations are not always rigorously supervised;

— valuable time is absorbed by administrative tasks which could be performed by people other than detectives;

— performance management systems are not fully developed in some forces.

BALANCING REACTIVE AND PROACTIVE WORK

65. A consequence of steeply rising workload, some duplication of effort and the tendency for detectives to get bogged down in paperwork is that the pattern of CID activity is highly reactive. The focus of effort is on the crime incident rather than the criminal. There is a cyclical process at work – the focus on crimes pulls officers away from the proactive work which is needed to identify and apprehend prolific criminals, who therefore carry on committing the crimes which generate the reactive burden for the police. A number of factors perpetuate this cycle, some of which are covered below, but it is also important to recognise that other parts of the criminal justice system may not always deter or stop prolific criminals from continuing to offend, contributing to this cycle.

CHANGES IN DETECTION TECHNIQUES

66. Traditional detection methods relied heavily upon the skills of individual detectives – the pursuit of enquiries, effective interviewing and interrogation, and running informants. These techniques are still important but they are no longer sufficient because, for example, the volume of reported crime means that officers have less time to spend in pursuit of enquiries on each investigation. In England and Wales the average caseload per officer (not just detectives) rose by 65% in the decade from 1982 to 1992 and has risen by 143% since 1970.

67. Good interviewing skills are often quoted as the area of expertise which most distinguishes detectives from their uniformed colleagues, and the restrictions on the conduct of interviews imposed by PACE have placed a premium on good interviewing techniques. But surprisingly few detectives have received specific training in interviewing skills – only 20% in the fieldwork sample – although a recent national initiative on investigative interviewing techniques will help in this area. Even where admissions are obtained, courts are increasingly unlikely to convict on the basis of confessions alone. Substantial corroboration is now needed and more suspects, particularly prolific criminals, have exercised their right to silence – that is, they have refused to provide information or answer questions put to them in interview knowing that the court would not be allowed to draw inferences from this[1].

68. Consequently there is a far greater imperative either to catch criminals in the act or to build a robust case against them after the crime has occurred, using evidence other than an admission. This evidence will be of two types – forensic (fingerprints, fibres, blood samples etc.) and intelligence-based. The police service's capacity to maintain clear-up levels in the light of changing circumstances is impaired by inadequate resourcing of the scientific support function and by a low level of proactive policing and intelligence gathering.

---

1 *Except where Section 2 of the Criminal Justice Act 1987 applies, empowering the Serious Fraud Office to compel interviewees to answer questions or risk a contempt charge. In a speech on 6 October 1993, the Home Secretary signalled an intention to amend the interpretation that may be made of silence by a suspect.*

69. The extraction of all available evidence from a scene relies not just upon the investigative actions of PCs and detectives, but also upon the work of scientific support staff such as SOCOs and fingerprint officers. In 1991 there were 1,135 SOCOs and 548 fingerprint officers, an increase of 16% and 19% respectively on the numbers employed in 1987, the year before the Commission reviewed the fingerprint service[1]. However, the number of notifiable offences increased by 40% over the same period. This expansion of workload has, in many forces, reduced the proportion of incidents attended by SOCOs and means that potential detections are being lost. For example, only 24% of cars which have been broken into are examined, a factor which contributes to the low level of clear-up for this crime.

70. The Commission's study on fingerprinting in 1988 estimated that 50% more identifications could be made by increasing the number of SOCOs and fingerprint officers to 75 per 100,000 notifiable offences. A follow-up review conducted as part of this study showed that there is still a marked shortfall against this figure, with four fifths of forces having fewer than 50 staff per 100,000 offences. Some variations in performance between forces were identified (Box E, overleaf).

71. In 1988 the Commission cited the limited use made of technology as one constraint. Automatic fingerprint recognition (AFR) increased the number of identifications by 100% when introduced in Scotland. It is particularly beneficial in carrying out 'cold searches' when there is no suspect against whom to check marks. It will only come on stream this year in England and Wales even though the basic technology has been available since the 1970s. Its introduction would have been delayed until 1996/97 if a consortium of forces had not been established to

---

1   *Improving the Performance of the Fingerprint Service, Police Paper No. 2 , HMSO 1988.*

Box E

VARIATIONS IN PERFORMANCE BETWEEN FORCES IN SCENES OF CRIME AND FINGERPRINT WORK

(i) **only about one in three relevant crime scenes were visited by SOCOs**, the average number of scenes visited being 800 per SOCO per year. However, the range varies from just over 450 in one force to around 1,350 in another. Reasons for a low number of visits include geographical factors, poor supervision and monitoring of SOCOs' schedules, and the requirement to do work other than visit scenes – in one force where SOCOs visited only around 500 scenes they spent 20% of their time installing police intruder alarms. Conversely, a very high number of visits should alert managers to assess whether SOCOs have sufficient time at each scene to conduct a thorough examination;

(ii) **the number of scenes at which marks were found** per SOCO ranged from a low of around 120 scenes per annum to almost 400 per annum. In 1991 one force collected marks from 50% of scenes examined, another in only 11% (see Exhibit below). A high percentage of non-productive visits should be a cause of concern, reflecting heavy workloads, inadequate monitoring of performance and a lack of guidance on the selection of scenes;

(iii) **the average number of identifications per fingerprint officer** in 1991 varied from fewer than 50 in four forces to more than 145 in the top ten performing forces. If the performance of all forces could be raised to the levels of the upper quartile, then the number of identifications would increase by 48%.

PERCENTAGE OF SCENE VISITS FROM WHICH MARKS ARE OBTAINED

The percentage of scenes visited by SOCOs which elicit marks ranges from 11% to 50% ...

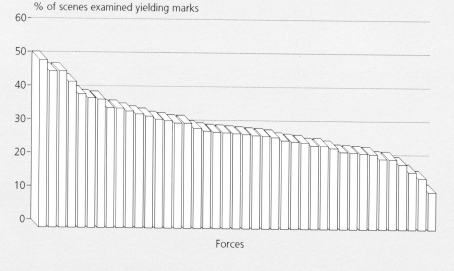

Source: Audit Commission analysis of 1991 data from the National Conference of Scientific Support

shortcut the planning period for the Home Office-sponsored system. There are many other equipment needs in the forensic field which are unmet; for example, only a handful of forces use the software package developed to monitor SOCO work and enhance the efficient use of scientific resources.

72. Scientific support has a low status, partly because staff are typically civilians and prevailing attitudes within the police accord civilians a lower status – irrespective of their job – than police officers. The effects of under-resourcing and low status are reinforced by organisational structures which place this function outside CID. At a day-to-day level, detectives rarely liaise with SOCOs on issues such as burglary *modus operandi*, the method used to gain entry to a house, or attend scenes alongside SOCOs. Their respective inputs are processed separately and in some cases are not matched up; in one of the study forces 31% of a sample of crime reports could not be matched up with a scene of crime report.

PROACTIVE POLICING AND INTELLIGENCE GATHERING

73. Only rarely does evidence from scientific support alone provide sufficient proof for detection, although it is often crucial for corroboration. The core of police work is the linking of evidence from the scene with information about likely offenders. However, detectives are in almost permanent 'fire-fighting' mode, handling a large number of individual cases and spending time going between the police station and scenes of crime. There is thus a low level of proactivity, that is co-ordinated work aimed at identifying and apprehending offenders, especially the more serious or prolific criminals. Proactive work is squeezed in when time permits, usually as part of a special initiative; it is rarely part of a planned programme. This is due in part to the fact that only a small fraction of available resources is commanded by the operational intelligence function – local intelligence officers (LIOs) who maintain the information databases, field intelligence officers (FIOs) who develop information into actionable intelligence, and crime pattern analysts.

74. The intelligence function has been the subject of three national studies in the last 20 years, the Baumber, Pearce and Ratcliffe reports[1]. Had they been implemented in full, there would be little further improvement to commend to forces. But some of the problems identified in these reports, on resource levels and status, still exist. There are an average of 13 LIOs per force, or one LIO for every 170 police officers[2]. The number of crime pattern analysts is not recorded separately but they tend to be far fewer in number than LIOs. There are an average of eight FIOs per force. In total, these key intelligence staff – LIOs, FIOs and crime pattern analysts – comprise just under 1% of total strength. In only one third of forces are there officers trained to deputise for all LIOs; without such provision intelligence analysis falters whenever the LIO is absent. LIOs face a constant struggle to avoid being drawn away from intelligence duties into other unrelated work – 40% suffer at least five such abstractions a month.

---

1   *Baumber: Report of the ACPO Sub-Committee on Criminal Intelligence, 1975.*
     Pearce: Report of the ACPO Working Party on a Structure of Criminal Intelligence Officers, 1978.
     Ratcliffe: Report of the ACPO Working Party on Operational Intelligence, 1986.

2   *Source: Audit Commission questionnaire.*

FIOs and surveillance teams

75. One important technique used against serious criminals is the compilation by field intelligence officers of intelligence 'packages'. A package contains all known relevant information about a target offender – description, accomplices, vehicles, favoured *modus operandi* – plus a tactical approach to securing arrest. It is followed up either by proactive units – *ad hoc* teams of officers with limited surveillance training – or by dedicated surveillance teams. Without a capacity to implement these packages with some form of surveillance or other operation, officers may become disillusioned or cynical about the value of intelligence work. However, such capacity is very limited. In the five study forces, with a total strength approaching 16,500, there were 43 FIOs and five surveillance teams (Table 2). The ratio of all officers to these proactive intelligence officers is 140:1.

Table 2
RESOURCES AVAILABLE TO SUPPORT PROACTIVE WORK

Force	A	B	C	D	E
Number of dedicated surveillance squads	2	1	0	0	2
Ratio of proactive* officers: detectives	1:14	1:24	1:58	1:25	1:19
Ratio of proactive* officers: all others	1:92	1:141	1:380	1:199	1:113
Average number of informants per DS/DC	2.8	1.6	1.7	1.1	2.2

*FIOs and surveillance team officers

Source: Audit Commission analysis of data from study forces

Quantifying costs and benefits

76. Running a surveillance team is undoubtedly a highly resource-intensive activity. Keeping track of a suspected criminal on the move requires eight to twelve officers, and four or more cars plus a motorcycle; with overheads this represents typical costs of around £2,500 for a ten-hour shift. Surveillance therefore has to be used very selectively, but is often the only way of establishing a case against professional criminals. However, around one quarter of forces do not have a dedicated surveillance team and all surveillance teams receive more requests than they can fulfil. Some officers respond to the lack of capacity by attempting surveillance activities themselves, but without the necessary training and equipment for the work they risk diminishing performance and revealing techniques which need to be kept secret.

77. The cost of surveillance can be calculated fairly readily, based upon an hourly rate for staff costs and overheads such as vehicles and equipment. However, in most forces there is little quantification of costs and only a few have attempted to quantify both costs and benefits. Gloucestershire has developed a system for assessing the value of possible surveillance operations using points ratings for key factors: the seriousness of the crime, the quality of intelligence, the clear-up potential, the calibre of the target (based on previous convictions), the likely recovery

of stolen property or drugs and an assessment of probable success. The total points score is converted into a financial sum which is then compared to the cost of mounting an operation. Whilst it cannot be totally precise and should not override professional judgement, such assessment can help both to target surveillance more effectively and to demonstrate its effectiveness.

THE STATUS OF INTELLIGENCE WORK

78. Resourcing is not the only issue to address; the status of intelligence officers is also important. Many LIOs, especially those with some CID experience, are highly effective but too often these posts are seen as the refuge of the lame, sick and elderly and rarely as a stepping-stone to advancement. The average LIO/FIO post-holder is 40 years old with 19 years service. Around half have no CID experience and 40% have not received specialist training.

79. Furthermore, IT support for intelligence work is inadequate. None of the study forces had a fully comprehensive computerised database which ensures that records are not duplicated (Exhibit 18). One of them has at least 57 manually maintained indices, in which the same criminal might appear a dozen times with different items of information that cannot easily be linked together. Some have a computerised nominal index, but if this is not integrated with other indices, such as vehicles, intelligence officers have a difficult task linking items of information together to form an overall picture. Without computerisation 'real time' searches of the records are impossible, the linking of crimes to criminals is extremely difficult and BCUs cannot easily share information or access the records.

Exhibit 18
AVAILABILITY OF INFORMATION TECHNOLOGY TO SUPPORT CRIME-RECORDING AND INTELLIGENCE
In the five study forces, there are a number of areas where computerisation is not available to ease data input and analysis ...

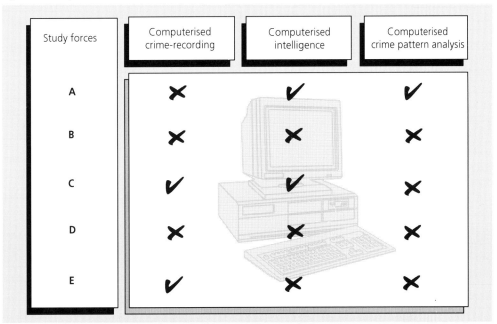

Study forces	Computerised crime-recording	Computerised intelligence	Computerised crime pattern analysis
A	✗	✔	✔
B	✗	✗	✗
C	✔	✔	✗
D	✗	✗	✗
E	✔	✗	✗

Source: Audit Commission analysis of information from study forces

80. Manual systems are labour-intensive to maintain, one estimate being that manual records require 40% more time to input than computer records, and are harder to weed i.e. delete dormant records. One of the country's smaller forces has 243,000 names in its nominal index compared to 87,000 names held by one of the metropolitan forces, suggesting that many records in the former system are out of date. Even where some or all of the intelligence indices are computerised, LIO effectiveness is impaired in many instances by the lack of clerical support, which ties the LIOs to a substantial inputting role when they should be driving the dissemination of the information.

81. Intelligence awareness amongst uniformed officers is variable. They are often cited by LIOs as potentially their most fruitful source of intelligence, but some officers contribute little or nothing to the intelligence pot. This is attributable in part to the poor calibre of some LIOs and the turgid nature of their intelligence bulletins. Additionally, the siting of the LIO's office away from the parade room, inadequate monitoring of intelligence forms which officers use to feed items of information into the system and a low priority given by sergeants to supervising this aspect of constables' work all contribute to the problem. Analysis of the number of intelligence forms submitted per officer reveals significant differences in the level of awareness and productivity of officers in feeding information into the systems. For example, two forces from the same general area and of almost identical size had submission ratios of 13 forms per officer and 43 per officer per year.

CRIME PATTERN ANALYSIS

82. Surveillance can be effective against the professional and serious criminal. A key technique which can be effective against prolific criminals is crime pattern analysis (CPA). Most crime reports are assigned to individual officers for investigation and thus the focus is on each crime incident. Yet a significant number of crimes against property, which account for 94% of crimes, are unlikely to be one-off occurrences but are rather multiple offences by a relatively small number of criminals. Crime pattern analysis is used to link together clusters or series of crimes such as burglaries on the basis of common characteristics – the means of entry, time of day that the crime occurred, type of items stolen and other features which, drawn together, constitute a criminal's hallmark. The point of establishing links is to attribute a series of crimes to one offender. It is rare to get sufficient evidence from one scene to secure a detection, but linked items of evidence from a number of scenes increase the odds against the criminal.

83. To be most effective CPA should be computerised and integrated with the crime-recording system so that large numbers of crime reports can be searched to identify possible patterns. Only 30% of forces benefit from such integration – at best, the rest have stand-alone CPA systems, which means that information about a crime has to be entered twice and is more difficult to network across the force area. Approximately half the provincial forces have some computerised CPA capacity at the local level, with a further 8% only having this capacity at headquarters. In the absence of a standard methodology, CPA systems in use will vary from force to force, which does not ease exchange of data between forces. None of the study forces had the benefit of a computerised, integrated system i.e. with every BCU linked to the same network across the force. Unless it is computerised and the information easily accessible via terminals to every BCU, its full value as a predictive technique and aid to targeting will not be realised.

INFORMANT HANDLING

84. Detectives often describe informants as 'the lifeblood of CID'. Whilst some may take a more cautious view of informants, and point to the difficulties inherent in recruiting informants, there is no doubt that they offer a very cost-effective source of detections. One force analysed the use over a recent six-month period of information from registered informants (payments can only be made to informants whose details have been vetted and registered with a senior officer). The results showed that £60 was paid out per person arrested and £57 per crime detected. For every £1 paid to informants, stolen property to the value of £12 was recovered. Some 219 crimes were cleared up at a cost for the period equivalent to one detective constable.

85. It is therefore surprising that detectives do not make more regular use of informants. Of those BCU-based detectives interviewed by the study team, 43% had no registered informants, 22% had just one, and only 17% had five or more. The overall average for DSs and DCs was just under two informants per detective. Uniformed officers also run informants and it is thus instructive to look at the overall ratio of officers to active informants i.e. those who have been paid for information within the last year. This ratio ranged from 7 officers per informant to 176 officers per informant in a force which had a large number of dormant informants. The register of informants needs regular evaluation to ensure that a reasonable proportion are still active; in a third of forces able to supply the information, fewer than 20% of registered informants received any payment in 1992.

86. There are several possible reasons for low use of informants. The amounts of money available for payments are relatively very small; the total amount disbursed to registered inform- ants in 1992 averaged £19,000 per force, with an average payment of £100. Another factor may be that the skill of cultivating informants has received relatively little emphasis in the didactic, law-based, foundation training courses for detectives. In some forces there is a disinclination to use them because of ethical problems – informants may have close connections with the criminal activities for which they are receiving payments to report on. Finally and perhaps most critically, recent interpretations of the rules governing disclosure of evidence make it more difficult to secure the anonymity of informants, and are likely further to restrict their use. Typically, forces will now offer no evidence and see a case be dropped rather than jeopardise the safety and future value of a reliable informant by disclosing his or her identity. In addition, any requirement to disclose other aspects of intelligence and targeting activities may also threaten their operational value; covert techniques cannot remain covert once they have been fully described in open court.

* * *

87. This chapter has highlighted the problems which forces face. They are not ones of commitment or competence on the part of individual officers, nor is there a lack of recognition that changes are needed. In a nutshell, because of a stark lack of technical support and some failures to implement modern management methods, the police are driven to fine-tuning a 1970s-based approach to crime investigation to tackle the 1990s volume of crime. They and the criminal justice system are almost overwhelmed by the volume of crime, and more and more of their effort is absorbed in day-to-day 'fire-fighting'. They have been drawn into a vicious circle

which they now need to break out of (Exhibit 19). What is needed is for each force to step back from the tyranny of the immediate pressures and take a strategic look at their overall management of crime investigation.

Exhibit 19
THE VICIOUS CIRCLE
The police and the rest of the criminal justice system are caught in a vicious circle of reactive policing in which crime threatens to overwhelm them ...

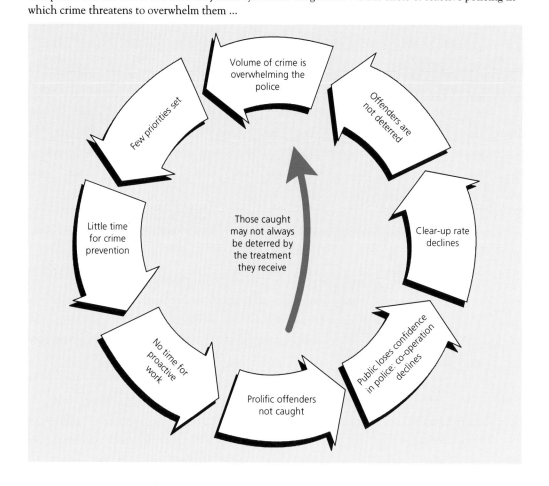

2. Improving Performance

88. To break free from the vicious circle and move into a virtuous circle in which detection levels improve, changes are required in the structures and processes used to tackle crime (Exhibit 20, overleaf). Forces need to:

— develop clearer management frameworks;

— make better use of existing resources;

— target the criminal and not just the crime.

The recommendations below suggest ways of implementing these elements, including a more rational allocation of resources to crime management; a more focused role for CID officers which makes the best use of their expertise; and greater emphasis on targeting prolific criminals.

DEVELOPING A CLEARER MANAGEMENT FRAMEWORK

89. A clear management agenda for the prevention and investigation of crime should:

— spell out the priority to be given to tackling crime in relation to other policing objectives, and clarify priorities *within* crime work;

— ensure crime management receives an appropriate share of resources;

— define a core role for detectives which makes the optimum use of their skills, and clarify other officers' responsibilities;

— ensure that structures are in place which help deliver policing objectives.

DETERMINING PRIORITIES

90. The demands made upon the police are increasingly varied and rising public anxiety about crime makes it imperative to clarify where crime management – i.e. the prevention and investigation of crime – sits in the hierarchy of policing objectives. ACPO's effort to define key operational areas was a useful start but did not identify peripheral activities which may need to be stripped out to release more resources to tackle crime. This is a contentious issue and will require both a strong lead from the Home Office and the understanding of the public to deliver a balanced response across all areas of policing. There are two equally critical stages to the process. The Home Office should spell out the core functions of policing, possibly using the Tripartite Forum[1] as a vehicle for discussion. Police authorities and their forces should then translate national objectives into local priorities, moderating and influencing public expectations of what it is feasible for the police to deliver.

91. If the police are given clearer priorities, as implied in the recent White Paper on Police Reform, there still remains a need to prioritise effort within the response to crime. This

---

1   *The Tripartite Forum meets two or three times a year to consider issues of mutual interest to the three parties to the tripartite structure: the Home Office, chief constables and police authorities.*

Exhibit 20

PROBLEMS, CAUSES AND SOLUTIONS IN CRIME MANAGEMENT

Forces need to address a range of problems in order to secure improvements in performance ...

PROBLEMS	CAUSES		SOLUTIONS

PROBLEMS

Lack of integrated approach to crime

Forces are not making the best use of resources

Focus is on crimes rather than criminals

CAUSES

- Police priorities not stated
- Crime prevention and investigation work separated
- Role of detectives unclear
- Uniformed officers do not take ownership of crime work
- Creeping parochialism in crime strategies

- Duplication of effort
- Officers lack technical support and equipment
- Supervision levels inadequate: lack of team-based approach
- Officers are bogged down with paperwork
- Performance management not robust

- Insufficient interview training
- Forensic potential not utilised
- Scientific support under-resourced
- Pattern of activity highly reactive
- Intelligence work has low status and is under-resourced
- Failure to exploit crime pattern analysis and informants

ACTION

SOLUTIONS

Develop clear management framework
- make policing priorities explicit
- clarify priorities within crime management
- define core role for CID and rationalise the division of labour with uniformed officers
- integrate all aspects of specialist crime work in a unified management structure
- clarify accountabilities at HQ and BCU levels

Make better use of resources
- establish crime desks
- improve quality of first response, to avoid duplication
- enhance investigative skills and supervision of uniformed officers
- introduce more teamwork and greater emphasis on supervision
- streamline administration
- undertake outcome analysis and develop suitable PI packages

Target the criminal
- develop intelligence strategy based on target criminals and communicate this to all officers
- enhance the intelligence and scientific support functions
- improve crime pattern analysis capacity
- build an element of proactivity into all detective duties
- encourage the use of informants

42

prioritisation may vary over time and from place to place, but there should be clear policies to determine the use of investigative resources at any given point. Factors influencing such policies would be:

— the nature of the offence;

— the likelihood of detection as a result of police effort;

— the vulnerability of the victim;

— the cost of the crime in question to the individual or the public;

— the frequency of the crime or the fact that it forms part of a series under investigation.

The relative priority given to crime prevention work is another key aspect of policy. The police are likely to remain the catalysts within the multi-agency partnership, but the contribution of the other agencies requires monitoring to ensure that the lack of a statutory framework does not reduce effort. The public should ensure that all reasonable steps are taken to seek crime prevention advice and put this into effect, particularly in respect of securing homes and vehicles and joining neighbourhood watch schemes. For their part, the police should address the problems of low status, relative under-resourcing, poor analytical capability and the remoteness from operational policing which currently blight crime prevention work within policing.

APPROPRIATE RESOURCES

92. Having defined the major problems, forces should ensure that resources are allocated in relation to needs. Forces with a low number of officers per 1,000 crimes (Exhibit 7, page 9) need to consider deploying more resources into crime management, either into CID or into crime response and investigation by uniformed officers, in order to improve their clear-up rate. The evidence suggests that *all* forces could benefit from assigning more resources to crime management since there is no indication of diminishing returns within the range of workloads currently facing forces (Exhibit 7). Without an overall increase, forces may find it hard to adopt the more resource-intensive, proactive approaches whilst maintaining commitments to quality of service to victims.

93. For the foreseeable future any increase in resources dedicated to crime management will probably have to be generated internally. There are three possible sources, of which the second and third may take a couple of years to implement:

— a management decision to redeploy existing resources, either generally into crime response and investigation or specifically into CID;

— a commitment to maximise the civilianisation of appropriate posts and assign the money saved to pay for police officers devoted to crime work. This will be made easier if current financial disincentives to civilianise are lifted by the Home Office, and budgetary flexibility is increased, as seems likely under the White Paper proposals. In 1992 HMIC estimated that some 6,500 police officers, 7% of strength, were occupying categories of post that could certainly be filled by civilians, termed 'category C posts', and the Audit Commission's previous studies have shown that many other categories of post are also suitable for partial civilianisation;

— scaling down top-heavy management structures. Although many forces have removed divisional tiers there remains wide variation between forces in management on-costs.

94. Civilian employment costs average around half those of police officers, so civilianising the conservative estimate of 6,500 key posts would generate resources sufficient for about another 3,250 officers. Combined with savings from streamlining management structures, this could generate the equivalent of up to 4,000 additional officers in provincial forces. If they devoted all their time to crime management, at current levels of productivity they could increase the number of clear-ups by about 126,000, raising the overall clear-up rate by almost three percentage points at current levels of crime.

Internal resource allocation

95. Resource allocation based on volume of crime contains no reward for successful crime reduction; if a BCU targets prolific offenders and enhances crime prevention work, resulting in a decline in reported crime, it could find itself penalised by losing officers. Given the diversity between forces in factors such as size, structure and geography it would be inappropriate to suggest one model of resource allocation for application in all forces. Some forces, such as Norfolk, already use a fairly rigorous approach. Police Paper No. 9[1] discussed the general approach:

— state what are relative priorities;

— specify the functions to be performed (demand drivers);

— establish the standards of service to be attained;

— calculate the average or expected task duration;

— use a formula to indicate each unit's share of resources;

---

1   *Reviewing the Organisation of Provincial Police Forces, HMSO, 1991.*

— fine-tune the allocations to take account of exceptional circumstances not represented by the formula.

DEFINING THE ROLE OF CID

96. Detectives are continually drawn into activities which fall outside their remit and clearer role definitions are needed, but without destroying the day-to-day flexibility which is particularly important in smaller forces. In utilising the expertise of detectives in dealing with serious crimes and prolific offenders, forces must avoid sending a signal to uniformed officers that they will be left with the dross of unsolvable or routine crime work. Forces should:

— **define a category of serious crime** which reflects both the complexity of the investigative task and the views of the public about the importance of the crime. It would be helpful to have national guidelines, agreed with the Home Office and ACPO. Once defined, the category of serious crime should be the principal responsibility of CID to investigate, although other factors may at times determine assignment of less serious crimes to a detective, such as the needs of the victim or the fact that these crimes form part of a series. This category can then be used as the basis for determining the relative size of a force's CID;

— **ensure that uniformed officers can deal competently** with crimes falling outside the serious category. Many forces have found that *ad hoc* teams of uniformed investigating officers are an effective response to this category of crime. Enhancing uniformed competence requires training, supervision, and setting investigative standards which identify tasks and expectations for particular types of crime. Detectives should have a consultancy and advisory role in relation to investigations by uniformed officers. This could entail, for example, advice on points of law and participation in prisoner interviews whilst preserving the investigative responsibilities of the uniformed officer.

GETTING THE STRUCTURE AND BALANCE OF RESOURCES RIGHT

97. Some forces, especially those where new structures are still bedding down, are experiencing problems in relationships between headquarters and basic command units. The solutions lie in:

— clearly defining new roles and responsibilities, including those of the small number of HQ-based detectives who have a strategic role;

— ensuring that the BCU commanders' accountabilities reflect both their management of all local response to crime *and* their corporate role, such as the response to crime which crosses BCU boundaries.

98. The clarification of responsibilities should incorporate the operation of the standing squads. Whilst the value of a squad approach to investigating certain types of crime – irrespective of where the offence occurred – is widely accepted, forces should determine whether these squads should generate much of their own workload or be expected directly to support BCUs. Some form of quasi-contractual service level agreement, such as those proposed by the Metropolitan Police and Thames Valley, may help. A formal statement, possibly agreed with BCU commanders, but at least communicated to them, of the objectives and detailed targets set for the squads, together with information about their performance, would be useful selling points. Careful consideration

should be given to tenure periods to ensure that an appropriate balance is struck between experience and the need for regular interchange (Exhibit 21).

Exhibit 21
MINIMUM TENURE IN SPECIALIST POSTS
The tenure period for specialist duties should take some account of the time taken in learning the job...

Specialist attachment	Time taken to become fully productive	Minimum tenure period
Fraud	12 months	4 years
HOLMES	12 months	4 years
Surveillance	6 months	2-3 years
Child abuse	6 months	2 years
Stolen vehicles	6 months	2 years
Intelligence	6 months	2 years
Cheque fraud	3 months	1 year
Drugs	3 months	1 year
Serious crime	N/A	N/A

Note: *'Time taken to become fully productive' is the period when officers are learning the basic elements of the job; during this period their operational effectiveness is limited. This should therefore be taken into account in determining minimum tenure periods to make best use of the investment in training. 'Minimum tenure period' is the length of time an officer should spend on specialist attachment so that overall 90% of time will have been fully productive .*

Source: *Audit Commission analysis, assisted by Northamptonshire Police*

Improving crime management at BCU level

99. At the BCU level, tensions exist in the new relationships between commanders and their detectives, especially where the commander has no CID experience. The course developed at the Police Staff College on investigation management for BCU commanders who do not have a background in CID work will alleviate but not solve such problems. A policy of more frequent interchange between CID and uniformed branch work should ensure that, over time, the number of commanders whose career is characterised by specialisation is reduced, but avoid the risk that detectives are de-skilled. For career planning it should be made clear that experience as a detective will enhance promotion prospects.

100. Accountability for tackling local crime will always rest with the BCU commander, but the role of the crime manager based in the BCU should be clarified. There is a strong case for giving the crime manager oversight of *all* crime work, including that undertaken by uniformed officers, where a BCU has:

— established a crime desk;

— formalised the criteria for allocation of cases to detectives or uniformed officers;

— set investigative standards for different crimes;

— clarified the nature of the supervision to be applied by uniformed sergeants over the quality of investigation by PCs.

MAKING BETTER USE OF RESOURCES

101. There are a number of areas where current good practice in some forces highlights the scope for improvement in others:

— establishing crime desks or crime management units;

— improving the quality of the first response;

— improving the management of investigations, specifically through more effective supervision, teamwork and better monitoring systems;

— improving systems for recording crime and streamlining the administrative process;

— providing managers with an information system which allows them to monitor workload, productivity, outcomes and cost-effectiveness.

ESTABLISHING CRIME DESKS

102. Effective crime management requires an appropriate and efficient initial response; prompt identification of cases meriting further investigation by detectives; integration of investigation, intelligence and scientific support inputs; and a high quality of communication with victims of crime. This represents a substantial task of co-ordination and progress-monitoring, and an increasing number of forces have adopted the crime desk mechanism to undertake it, especially in urban areas with a large volume of reported crime. The precise form and size of crime desks vary but the essential feature is that all crime reports pass through the crime desk for analysis, quality assurance of the initial response, and monitoring of follow-up investigation.

103. Not all reports of crime receive, or may warrant, an officer's attendance. However, minor and virtually undetectable crime still affects the victim, whose needs feature prominently in quality of service initiatives. Forces are therefore striving to give victims of minor crime an acceptable quality of service whilst at the same time using resources to best effect. In some forces, the crime desk has been used as the first response to some crimes. In Norfolk this concept is incorporated in an advice line. Here, amongst other duties, officers deal with between 30%-40% of all crime reports over the telephone and the control room dispatches officers to attend the remaining incidents. Callers are also given advice related to the crime, for example on securing a car after a theft; this has helped to ensure high levels of public satisfaction with the crime desk. The average time spent responding to a telephone call and completing a crime report is 17 minutes, compared to one hour when an officer attends. The Home Office Police Research Group has calculated that the unit saved 2,600 officer hours per year in the main BCU where the scheme operates.

104. Resistance to this approach is based upon assumptions that the public will not be satisfied solely with telephone contact even where the crime is relatively minor. But quality of service to victims does not have to suffer. South Yorkshire evaluated a long-running pilot crime desk and found user satisfaction levels of 84%, compared to 70% where crime victims were visited by a police officer. Those reporting crime often find it inconvenient to wait for a visit when the officer only records details which could have been given over the telephone; those who expect a visit may do so because they are unaware of alternative means of reporting crimes. The crime desk has the important advantage of providing one contact point for crime victims. Forces could therefore benefit from publicising better the options available and influencing expectations to align with what is achievable. The impact upon investigative performance has not been rigorously evaluated in many forces, but there is no discernible trend of decline in the number of offences cleared up after the introduction of crime desks. An improvement in detection performance will depend upon forces making the most effective, crime-related use of the resources released as a result of crime desks, but some encouragement can be drawn from Hampshire's experience (Box F).

Box F
CRIME DESK CASE STUDY

> Hampshire established a version of the crime desk concept in January 1991 which linked initial response to follow-up enquiries, concentrating upon property crime. After rigorous evaluation the model was introduced throughout the force in the following year.
>
> **(i) Objectives**
>
> The two objectives were to improve quality of service to victims of property crime and increase detections in this category; in both aspects the force was dissatisfied with its previous achievement levels. Success was to be monitored by crime and detection figures and by quarterly public surveys.
>
> **(ii) Organisation**
>
> The unit is staffed from 8.00am to 10.00pm Monday to Saturday using a team of eight officers in total, drawn from the sub-divisional CID strength. At any one time two officers staff the crime desk, taking all reports of property crime and assessing the appropriate response. Staffing of the desk is rotated weekly amongst the whole team. The other six officers form an investigation team, although of course not all will be on duty at any one time.
>
> **(iii) Crimes and detections**
>
> The number of crimes reported increased after the unit was set up; this is typical and reflects public awareness of the facility and ease of reporting, and confidence by other police officers that these crimes will be dealt with more competently. The number of detections for property crime increased by 31% in the first evaluation period.
>
> **(iv) Public attitudes**
>
> The victim surveys showed that before the unit was established satisfaction levels with police efforts averaged 61%; this rose to 75% after the unit began operating. Victim satisfaction with follow-up information about the progress of the investigation rose from 23% to 30%.

IMPROVING THE QUALITY OF THE FIRST RESPONSE

105. Forces need to improve the quality of the first response to reported crime, through more rational deployment of officers and higher standards of investigation at the scene. A more efficient and effective response to the high-volume crime of burglary can be secured by one person in one visit, followed where appropriate by screened attendance of other officers rather than the three or four automatic, separate visits which characterise the traditional response (Exhibit 22). The initial response could be by a detective or a specialist scene visit officer, ensuring that expertise

Exhibit 22
GETTING IT RIGHT AT THE FIRST VISIT
Many of the tasks undertaken at the scene of a burglary could be carried out in one visit ...

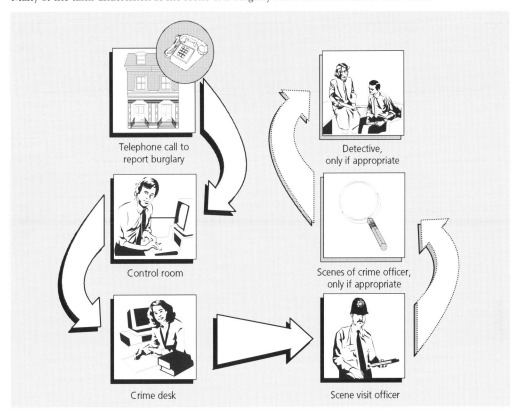

Telephone call to
report burglary

Control room

Crime desk

Detective,
only if appropriate

Scenes of crime officer,
only if appropriate

Scene visit officer

is applied to the task in the critical early stage when evidence is relatively fresh. If the first response remains the uniformed PC, this officer should work to an agreed standard of investigation and be given sufficient time to complete the work before being deployed to another incident. A common format for crime reports, which officers could be trained to complete to a prescribed standard, could aid consistency, supervision and the transfer of information between forces. However, differences in IT systems may impede such standardisation.

106. The officer allocated to the scene visit is most likely to be a uniformed constable or a detective, followed in some or the majority of instances by a SOCO, but a number of permutations are possible. For example, West Yorkshire uses a mix of detectives and uniformed officers who have had brief attachments to CID, whilst Surrey has recently launched a burglary initiative which deploys a detective and SOCO working in pairs as the first officers on the scene. Dyfed-Powys has trained a number of PCs and DCs in basic scenes of crime techniques, freeing SOCOs for more selective visits.

107. There are important advantages with the streamlined approach. Firstly, the amount of information gleaned from the initial visit is maximised and it is less likely that the scene will go cold whilst the force organises repeat visits. Minimising the duplication of effort entailed in the more traditional approach produces savings in officer time and thus cost (Table 3). If redeployed into crime-related work these additional resources could lead to around 26,000 more clear-ups per year in provincial forces in England and Wales. The need for early and systematic extraction of

intelligence is addressed; this helps to identify whether the crime forms part of a series or pattern upon which CID effort can be focused. Cases where there are no fruitful leads can be filed at an early stage without involving detectives. Finally, the demands made upon the victim are minimised.

Table 3
RESOURCE SAVINGS FROM STREAMLINED APPROACH

Force	A	B	C	D	E	**Total**
Number of officers saved	19	23	9	5	45	101
£million	0.57	0.69	0.27	0.15	1.35	3.03

Source : Audit Commission analysis of data from five study forces

108. The streamlined scene visit and the crime desk concept are closely linked. In forces which do not use a crime desk, certain improvements in police response to a crime incident can still be made. Command and control room operators should be given guidelines for the duration of attendance at the scene, backed by training and supervision in their application, so that officers are allowed a reasonable time to complete the tasks before being directed to another incident. Shift patterns of control room staff and SOCOs could be better geared to match peaks in demand. Operators could negotiate with callers a higher proportion of non-urgent responses. This would allow more timetabled programmes of visits by police officers and SOCOs. Uniformed constables require better training in the key tasks at the scene; and the supervisory responsibilities of sergeants in respect of scene attendance and completion of crime reports should be emphasised and monitored.

109. Some argue that the streamlined approach is not appropriate for their force because the public expect the pattern of emergency uniformed response followed by SOCO and CID attendance. The Commission's survey of burglary and autotheft victims revealed that only around 20% report their burglary via the 999 emergency system, the majority telephoning the police station on an ordinary line or calling at the station in person. Approximately half the victims did not expect the police to treat the burglary report as an emergency. This suggests that the police have rather more flexibility than is currently assumed in how they respond, and can avoid some of the problems associated with sending the first available officer to the scene.

110. Forces have the opportunity to influence public expectations by, for example, publicising what response the force will provide in given situations, either in a charter-type document or by way of published service standards. Whilst the victims of burglary and other serious crimes should always be visited by the police, a message to the public – perhaps from the Home Office – concerning other situations where officer attendance may not be appropriate could help in aligning expectations with police capacity. The public can assist the police by taking a reasonable view of the circumstances where officer attendance is not necessary.

IMPROVING THE MANAGEMENT OF INVESTIGATIONS

111. A number of improvements in the management of resources are possible. Firstly, the key supervisory skills required for the role of DS, which are likely to include leadership and motivation, understanding of the principles of delegation, project management and performance

appraisal, should be identified. Assessment of these skills, or the potential for their acquisition, can then be incorporated into selection and promotion procedures. All newly appointed DSs – and existing DSs as appropriate – should receive basic training in these key supervisory skills.

112. A critical point in improving supervision is that the personal caseload of DSs should reflect the fact that contributing to and supervising other officers' work is a principal role. In some instances this would entail a reduction in DSs' personal caseloads and more direction of team-based investigations. Complex cases will still require the expertise of a DS. Where forces can move to larger teams, some DSs not needed in team-leader roles could operate as senior investigators. More effective supervision of investigations, probably by using a facilitative style rather than 'standing over the shoulders', should extend to more formal procedures for allocation. For example, a DS could specify, perhaps in writing, the lines of enquiry to be pursued and how these enquiries are to be undertaken, with indications of expected timescale. It should be standard practice to record on the case file the supervisor's comments about the progress and conclusion of the investigation.

113. DSs should oversee elements of the investigative process – the use of intelligence sources, interviews with witnesses and suspects, giving evidence in court – and not just the end product i.e. the crime file. The DS should, though, advise on complex cases and systematically review a sample of prosecution files before they are submitted to the ASU or CPS. The same point applies to uniformed sergeants supervising the work of PCs. Dip-sampling of interviews by other officers, such as detective inspectors or superintendents, should be conducted systematically, using a pro forma to record the assessment, and should address both compliance with PACE and the quality of interrogation.

EFFECTIVE TEAMWORK AND CASE ALLOCATION

114. There could be benefit in placing a greater emphasis on team-based investigation. Teamwork facilitates the sharing of information and allows the team-leader to utilise individual

strengths. Rather than performing all tasks in one investigation, officers can develop specialisations such as interviewing or intelligence gathering. The team's investigative activities can be more easily targeted towards offenders, which is more resource-intensive than undertaking investigation at the scene of a crime and requires a high degree of co-ordination. And finally, there will be far fewer continuity problems of the type which arise when an officer is on leave or abstracted.

115. Currently, the typical size of CID teams is one DS and three or four DCs. Following its comprehensive review of crime investigation (the Crime Investigation Priority Project), the Metropolitan Police moved to team-based investigation based on groups of one DS, four DCs and two trainee investigators. The trainee investigators are trained to a standard which, although not as rigorous as that received by detective constables, is superior to that received by many CID aides (uniformed officers on attachment to CID but not filling a substantive post). The trainee investigators take responsibility for less complex investigations and work with DCs and the DS on more serious cases.

116. Some form of computerised allocation and case-tracking system should be in place in all forces; at present DSs try to keep a lot of this detail in their heads. A more formal system would bring case files to the DS's attention, say every seven days, for a review of progress and filing where leads have been exhausted, and provide 'at a glance' details of the status of cases. At the suggestion of the study team, investigation logs are currently being piloted in one of the study forces; if successful, these will provide useful information for supervisors about the length of time spent per investigation and the type of activities undertaken, which can then be linked to the case outcome.

RESOURCING AND INTEGRATING SUPPORT FUNCTIONS

117. Teamwork should integrate intelligence, crime pattern analysis and scientific support staff more effectively with detectives, ensuring that these functions are less the poor cousins of investigation and more the equal partners. Placing these various activities under a unified management structure could help, as could more emphasis on them in detective training courses. More significantly, efforts should be made to raise the status of these functions; for example, through the calibre of the people appointed to them – spreading talent around rather than concentrating it in the more traditional elite areas.

118. But perhaps the hardest decisions are those involving resource priorities. Making information technology and other equipment a priority for investment will enhance investigative effectiveness to a greater degree than providing additional officers for general patrol. The most pressing needs are for more vehicles, secure radios, forensic equipment and specialist computerised systems such as HOLMES II, which updates the existing HOLMES system and is less resource-intensive. The Home Office and ACPO are preparing an IT strategy for the police service which will establish minimum national standards and identify how best IT can contribute to developments in operational policing. The pressure from the public to plough more resources into visible patrol is recognised, but there needs to be greater awareness that, whatever impact they may have in reducing anti-social behaviour and increasing public reassurance, more bobbies on the beat have relatively little impact on crime detection. On the other hand, 'technological fixation', seeing IT as a panacea for all ills, is a risk that must be avoided.

119. The problems caused by a long period of inflexibility in financing arrangements are recognised in the recent White Paper, which proposes greater discretion for chief constables in how money should be spent. The cumbersome approval procedure for equipment and major capital spending should certainly be streamlined[1]. The current variation between forces in the availability of technical support will need to be taken into account before the government locks forces into a new regime of formula funding and outcome assessment. National minimum standards of provision could be determined by Her Majesty's Inspectorate of Constabulary and forces brought up to these standards through a transitional capital fund.

STREAMLINING ADMINISTRATION TO REDUCE NON-PRODUCTIVE TIME

120. The time constraints and quality demands laid down recently by the Crown Prosecution Service have caused some officers to reconsider the file preparation process. The consensus amongst those detectives interviewed is that centralised administrative support units, staffed by a mix of police officers and civilians, are useful for the bulk of less complex cases and traffic offences, normally dealt with by uniformed officers. More complex committal files, likely to be used at trials, should, many argue, be prepared by detectives under supervision. However, this would keep detectives desk-bound and unable to pursue investigations. Forces should consider making local administrative and clerical support available, to complement the services which ASUs can provide. Many detectives critical of the current system were working in offices miles from their nearest ASU, with the logistical and communications problems this entails. Almost 40% of detectives interviewed stated a preference for some form of local office support. An advantage of larger BCUs – i.e. over 250 officers – is that they are more able to sustain their own ASU, enhancing local accountability and accessibility.

121. The whole issue of the administrative burden has recently been examined by the Home Office[2], and improvement cannot come too soon. In the five study forces alone the preparation of typed summaries of taped interviews costs in the region of £1.5 million per year in detective time. The need for streamlining the paperwork trail imposed on police officers may require a review of the demands imposed by the CPS, such as deadlines for file submission, the requirement for full files when a guilty plea has been entered, acceptability of tape summaries prepared by civilians, stipulations about typed documentation, and the responsibility for witness warning. Where technology permits, a force should be able to submit a case file on disk, with the duplication of hard copy items then a matter for the CPS. Finally, there is an urgent need to rationalise procedures for calling officers to attend the courts; Suffolk has recently agreed a system which has reduced the wasted time spent waiting at court.

IMPROVING PERFORMANCE MANAGEMENT SYSTEMS

122. In many forces improvements in performance management are impeded by inadequacies in information technology. However, there are issues which forces can address irrespective of the state

---

1   *The Audit Commission recommended this change in Footing the Bill, Police Paper No. 6, 1990.*

2   *Opportunities for Reducing the Administrative Burdens on the Police, Police Research Series, Paper No. 3, London, Home Office, 1993.*

of their IT system. One is the need for a suitable mix of qualitative and quantitative information to allow internal evaluation of performance at all stages of crime prevention and investigation (Exhibit 23). The deficiencies of using the overall detection rate as the bell-wether indicator are well rehearsed. Of other available indicators, the number of primary clear-ups per officer is the most robust one for comparing performance between forces. Its main drawback is that detectives may be tempted to produce good figures from relatively minor crime, rather than tackling the more serious crimes where their *apparent* productivity may be less impressive.

123. More robust measures may need to be based upon weighted categories of crime, with the weighting factor reflecting the complexity and seriousness of the crime. As an example, for performance measurement purposes only, a shoplifting detection might be attributed a weighting of 20, compared to 200 for a burglary detection and 450 for an armed robbery clear-up. It may also be appropriate to weight the method of clear-up and type of offender, with arrests and charges of serious or prolific offenders attracting a higher weighting than a first-time offender. A different approach to crime categorisation in the Home Office's compiled statistics could also be considered. One possible alternative to the current system, grouping categories of crime according to seriousness and complexity of investigation, is outlined in Appendix 2. For the performance appraisal of individual detectives, qualitative aspects are critical. These need to be reflected in a mix of process and outcome indicators, looking not just at clear-ups but also the quality of interviewing, extraction and use of intelligence and the management of informants.

BRINGING GOOD PRACTICE TOGETHER

124. A mechanism which can draw together all the elements set out above is the crime management unit. This develops the basic concept of the crime desk into a unit which, under the direction of the crime manager and based upon intelligence and CPA, drives the whole crime management process at BCU level. It is not predominantly an administrative function, although it does perform some administration e.g. communicating with victims. Rather, it sets and monitors standards to ensure that officers undertake high-quality investigations; provides a clear focus for decisions on individual cases; links investigation at the scene with further enquiries, intelligence work and post-arrest activities such as the conduct of searches; and finally co-ordinates the scientific support, intelligence, crime prevention and investigative functions to ensure that crime management is a coherent rather than compartmentalised process (Exhibit 24, page 56).

TARGET THE CRIMINAL AND NOT JUST THE CRIME

125. The fundamental objective in recommending a clearer management framework, a review of resource levels and measures which make better use of resources, is to generate a capacity for proactive work which targets prolific and serious criminals. A relatively small number of individuals account for a substantial proportion of detected crime. Analysis of the histories of a large sample of males born in a particular year showed that 7% of them accounted for 65% of all convictions in this age group[1]. The dictum that effective policing targets the criminal rather than the crime is familiar to all detectives. They maintain, however, that they are frustrated in this ambition by the weight of crime, which absorbs all but a fraction of available time. Adoption of

---

1   *Home Office Statistical Bulletin 32/89.*

Exhibit 23

WORKLOAD INFORMATION AND PERFORMANCE INDICATORS – ILLUSTRATIVE

A mix of qualitative and quantitative measures for internal monitoring of workload and performance could be developed from the following illustrative indicators ...

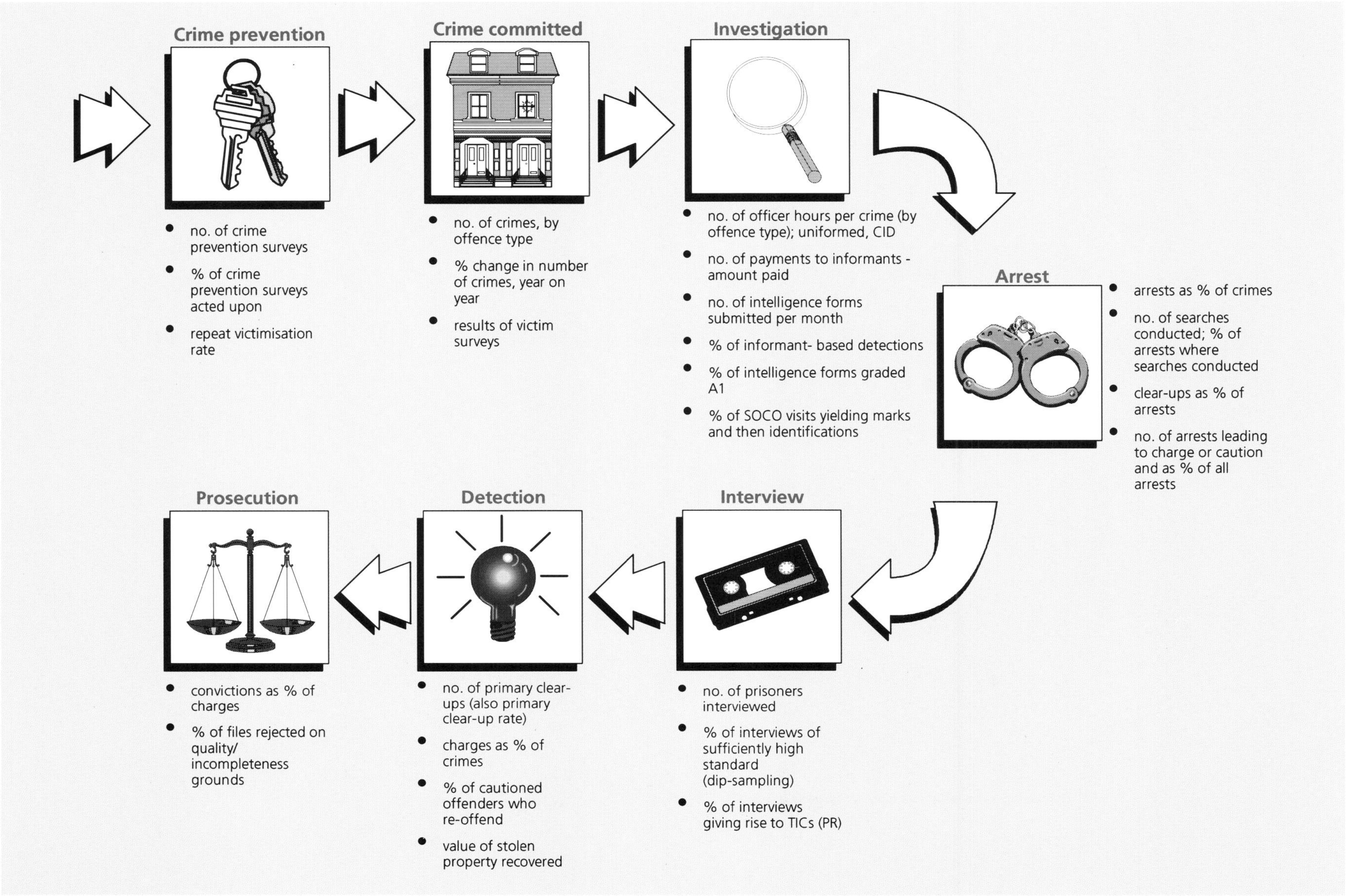

Crime prevention

- no. of crime prevention surveys
- % of crime prevention surveys acted upon
- repeat victimisation rate

Crime committed

- no. of crimes, by offence type
- % change in number of crimes, year on year
- results of victim surveys

Investigation

- no. of officer hours per crime (by offence type); uniformed, CID
- no. of payments to informants - amount paid
- no. of intelligence forms submitted per month
- % of informant- based detections
- % of intelligence forms graded A1
- % of SOCO visits yielding marks and then identifications

Arrest

- arrests as % of crimes
- no. of searches conducted; % of arrests where searches conducted
- clear-ups as % of arrests
- no. of arrests leading to charge or caution and as % of all arrests

Interview

- no. of prisoners interviewed
- % of interviews of sufficiently high standard (dip-sampling)
- % of interviews giving rise to TICs (PR)

Detection

- no. of primary clear-ups (also primary clear-up rate)
- charges as % of crimes
- % of cautioned offenders who re-offend
- value of stolen property recovered

Prosecution

- convictions as % of charges
- % of files rejected on quality/ incompleteness grounds

55

Exhibit 24
CRIME MANAGEMENT UNITS
The crime management unit extends the basic crime desk approach to bring together the various elements of crime prevention, response, intelligence and investigation...

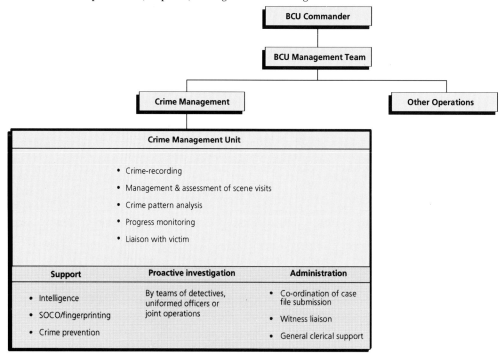

the measures laid out above should relieve some of this pressure, but freed time should be focused on criminal targets. This requires a clear intelligence strategy, communicated to all officers, and an enhanced intelligence function. It is also essential that proactive work, especially surveillance, is subject to a rigorous mechanism for objective-setting and evaluation of outcomes to ensure that its use is appropriate and cost-effective. Surveillance and informant-handling need to be conducted within ethical guidelines which give due recognition to the civil liberties issues which their use raises, but the proposals in this report do not breach the existing framework of individual liberties.

BETTER USE OF INTELLIGENCE AND CRIME PATTERN ANALYSIS

126. If the intelligence function is not adequately resourced, staffed by committed officers with good communication skills and managed in an integrated way, then the scope for proactive policing is considerably diminished. A number of steps could be taken to improve the current situation.

127. Firstly, the bedrock of intelligence work is the contribution from uniformed officers. A commitment to intelligence gathering in operational policing needs to be continually reinforced by senior officers, for example through appraisal. Secondly, forces should ensure that they resource the intelligence function with an adequate number of officers plus appropriate clerical support. All LIOs should have colleagues trained to deputise for them in their absence and, wherever possible, BCUs should each have a Field Intelligence Officer. Thirdly, management should ensure that parochialism is not allowed to impair intelligence flows across the force; some forces have determined that intelligence is a central function, with staff decentralised to BCUs. Finally, the status of intelligence officers should be improved through policy commitments by chief officers and the nature of appointments. Forces should be prepared to put their best and brightest officers into intelligence and train them in the specialist skills required.

128. These points focus upon human resources, but there are unmet needs in technical support for proactive policing. Police forces hold many thousands of intelligence records, grouped in categories or indices for criminals, vehicles used by criminals, methods used to commit crimes and so on. To be used most effectively these should be on a computerised database, accessible from every BCU on a 24-hour-a-day basis. After computerising its intelligence records and making them easily accessible, Dorset found that officers began using the system more frequently and the number of intelligence forms submitted rose tenfold. There should be only one record for each name in the index, easily linked to crime, vehicle and other indices. Crime pattern analysis should be incorporated into all crime management systems at BCU level. This requires a higher priority for equipment and training for this activity. It is currently applied principally for CID use in linking crimes, but it potentially has wider applications in directing and focusing uniformed patrol towards crime 'hot spots' by, for example, analysis of data on incidents reported to control rooms. Work is under way in the Home Office to establish a standard specification for local CPA applications.

PROACTIVE POLICING

129. Intelligence-led, proactive policing operates at three main levels. Even the smallest forces need access to a surveillance capacity if they are to derive full benefit from targeting and meet the pressures created by serious criminals operating across force boundaries. Formerly, forces could call upon Regional Crime Squads to tackle such criminals, but their focus is now upon a relatively small number of criminals operating at a national level. Less resource-intensive are specialist squads, whose work should be directed principally at target criminals who cross BCU boundaries. Thirdly, within BCUs *ad hoc* proactive teams and a proportion of mainstream CID activity should be directed towards local targets such as prolific burglars. Proactive initiatives at BCU level should be integral to the work of CID, directed by the DI or DS and fed by a detailed understanding of crime patterns and active criminals (Box G, overleaf). Every BCU officer should, for example, know who are the top ten local target offenders.

ENCOURAGING THE USE OF INFORMANTS

130. The emphasis given in this report to more proactive styles of working, greater teamwork and concentration upon the more serious and complex crimes means that law-based training needs to be supplemented with skills-based approaches emphasising intelligence and informant-handling. One aspect of the enhanced supervisory role for DSs should be to encourage detectives first to cultivate informants and then task them to produce information on high-priority crimes or criminals. Forces should also review the current budgets for informants and ensure that officers are aware of the cost-efficiency of informants. Senior officers should recognise that the tendency always to try and drive down the level of payment requested by informants may be counter-pro-ductive in the long term if it disinclines informants to co-operate with the police. Management information on informant use could be much improved: Northamptonshire has developed a simple software package which provides monthly information on contacts with informants, items of information, arrests, property recovered etc. 'Crimestopper' schemes, whereby members of the

The value of crime pattern analysis and a targeted approach is illustrated by Operation Bumblebee, a burglary initiative launched by the Metropolitan Police and later adopted by several provincial forces. The operation is driven by intelligence and CPA, and a combination of tactics are used – targeting of handlers, regular searches of the houses of known active burglars, cultivation of informants and so on. The initiative has been publicised across London to get over the message that, far from giving up on burglary, the police have launched a powerful attack on it.

The results are impressive. In the first year, an increase in burglary reports of 18% over the previous year was stemmed to a 2% rise, and the following year burglaries dropped by 7%. The clear-up rate has more than doubled. Whilst aware of the risk of displacement, the force does not believe there has been a significant shift of criminal activity over divisional boundaries.

public can be paid for information on a confidential basis, have proved successful in some force areas, but in others the response could be improved through better publicity. Such schemes may, however, reduce people's willingness to be a registered informant.

* * *

131. Although the majority of recommendations contained within this report are directed towards the police, the role of other parties can be quite influential in bringing about improvements. A summary of the report's recommendations for police forces and these other parties is set out below.

132. This report has attempted to analyse why the police find themselves caught in a vicious circle in which their best efforts are not succeeding in bringing crime under control. The police alone cannot solve the crime problem but they can tackle it more effectively. Cultural attitudes within the service need to change, and current practices and levels of technical support need to be improved to equip the police better to deal with the tasks confronting them. Changes at the margin will not be sufficient; the police need to put more resources into fighting crime, make their priorities more explicit, adopt modern management methods and give greater emphasis to targeting offenders. Along with changes elsewhere in the criminal justice system, this would help

to increase detections, raise clear-up rates significantly, and move from the vicious circle into a virtuous circle in which ultimately crime could be brought under control (Exhibit 25).

Exhibit 25
THE VIRTUOUS CIRCLE
Clearer prioritisation, emphasis on prevention and more resources moved into proactive work could produce a virtuous circle...

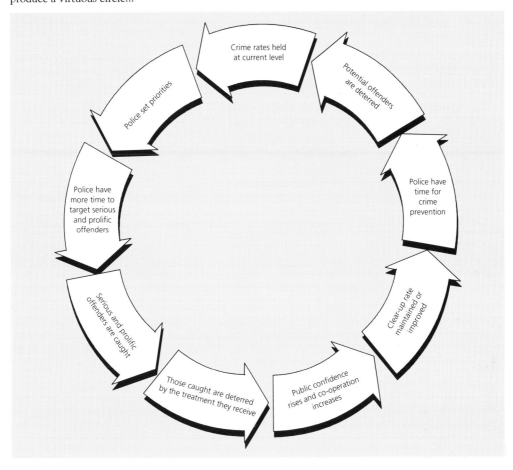

For the Home Office:

(i)   Identify the core functions of policing, reconciling public expectations with what it is feasible for the police to deliver (paragraph 90).

(ii)   Consider the need to strengthen multi-agency partnership responsibilities for crime prevention work (paragraph 91).

(iii)   Remove the current financial disincentive to civilianise key posts and provide financial or other incentives to scale down top-heavy management structures in forces (paragraph 93).

(iv)   Establish guidelines for a standard definition of 'serious crime' (paragraph 96) and better categorisation of crimes generally (paragraph 123).

(v)   Explain to the public where attendance by the police at an incident may not be appropriate (paragraph 110).

(vi)   Facilitate the provision of adequate technical support to front-line officers by streamlining procedures for equipment purchasing (paragraphs 118 to 119).

(vii)   Take steps to help reduce the administrative burden upon operational police officers (paragraph 121).

For police authorities:

(i)   Work with police forces on translating core policing activities into local priorities so that the service reflects local needs (paragraph 90).

(ii)   Strengthen the multi-agency approach to crime prevention (paragraph 91).

(iii)   Encourage civilianisation to free officers for operational work (paragraph 93).

For other parts of the criminal justice system:

(i)   If possible, clarify the circumstances in which the identity of an informant is to be disclosed (paragraph 86).

(ii)   Review the demands made upon police officers by the requirements of Pre-Trial Issues, specifically the need for full files in all cases where a guilty plea has been entered, the deadlines imposed for file submission, the typing and copying of documents, preparation of taped interview summaries, and location of responsibility for tasks such as witness warning (paragraph 121).

(iii)   Ensure that court procedures minimise unproductive waiting time at court by police officers (paragraph 121).

For individual members of the public:

(i)   Ensure that all reasonable steps are taken to seek crime prevention advice and put this advice into effect, particularly in respect of securing homes and vehicles, joining watch schemes etc. (paragraph 91).

(ii)   Adopt a reasonable view of circumstances where attendance by a police officer may be neither necessary nor an efficient use of police time (paragraph 110).

For police forces:

(i)   Make explicit what priority is attached to crime management within force objectives (paragraph 90); enhance the status of crime prevention (paragraph 91).

(ii) Clarify the basis for resource allocation decisions across the range of force activities; consider redeployment of resources into the crime function (paragraphs 92 to 94).

(iii) Define the role of CID and ensure that detectives are deployed in ways which make the best use of their expertise (paragraph 96).

(iv) Clarify the accountabilities of officers for crime management; in particular, resolve any ambiguities arising from new force structures and the ending of dual accountability (paragraphs 97 and 98).

(v)   Consider the establishment of crime desks, or their expansion into crime management units as appropriate (paragraphs 102 and 124).

(vi) Take steps to eliminate duplication of effort in the initial response to crimes such as burglary and seek to improve the quality of investigative work conducted as part of the initial response (paragraphs 105 and 108).

(vii) Strengthen the supervision of investigations at BCU level, through appropriate training, adjustments to caseload, establishment of larger investigative teams and case monitoring systems (paragraphs 111 to 116).

(viii) Develop closer links between investigation and support functions such as intelligence; ensure that these functions are adequately resourced (paragraphs 117 to 119).

(ix) Consider whether Pre-Trial Issues requires adjustments to current ASU and file management systems, in particular the provision of administrative support within local CID offices (paragraph 120).

(x)   Consider methods of weighting crime clear-ups within the context of a more comprehensive performance management system (paragraphs 122 and 123).

(xi) Enhance the resourcing of the intelligence function; if not with additional resources, then with higher-calibre staff and improved technological support, as appropriate (paragraphs 127 and 128).

(xii) Through more effective use of resources – and where appropriate redeployment of resources – generate a capacity at both force-wide and BCU level for a greater degree of proactive work, targeting prolific and serious criminals (paragraph 129) and encouraging the use of informants (paragraph 130).

Appendix 1

MEMBERSHIP OF ADVISORY PANEL AND STUDY WORKING GROUP

The Advisory Panel consists of members of the Association of Chief Police Officers (ACPO) who meet with officers and members of the Commission at regular intervals to discuss and advise upon the police studies programme. The members are:

Mr David Blakey, Chief Constable, West Mercia Constabulary

Mr David Burke, Chief Constable, North Yorkshire Police

Mr Albert Pacey, former Chief Constable, Gloucestershire Constabulary (now Director-General of the National Criminal Intelligence Service)

Mr Brian Weight, Chief Constable, Dorset Police

Mr Peter Winship, Assistant Commissioner, Metropolitan Police

A working group provided invaluable advice to the study team. They participated with the permission of their forces but expressed their views on a personal basis:

Detective Chief Inspector Gary Copson, Metropolitan Police

Inspector Graham Hartshorn, South Yorkshire Police

Chief Superintendent David Lambert, Kent County Constabulary

Superintendent Geoff Nicholls, Cheshire Constabulary

Detective Chief Superintendent Geoff Ogden, Humberside Police

Detective Chief Superintendent Chris Page, Sussex Police

Detective Chief Superintendent John Saunders, Her Majesty's Inspectorate of Constabulary (now returned to Suffolk Constabulary)

Chief Superintendent Andrew Timpson, Northamptonshire Police

Assistance was also provided at key stages of the study by Chief Superintendent Ian Blair of the Metropolitan Police.

Appendix 2

CRIME CATEGORISATION

The Home Office produces a large volume of statistics each year on crimes and criminals which are invaluable for research into, for example, long-term trends and profiles of offenders. However, the methodology for data collection and presentation poses some problems for evaluation of police performance because crimes are only partially differentiated on the basis of seriousness and complexity, and each crime has the same statistical weighting within the overall clear-up rate.

HOME OFFICE MAIN GROUPINGS OF OFFENCES:

(1) **Violence against the person** – including murder, manslaughter, causing death by reckless driving, wounding and assault;

(2) **Sexual offences** – including rape, indecent assault, procuration and indecency between males;

(3) **Burglary** – in both dwellings and other property, and including attempted burglary;

(4) **Robbery** – all theft accompanied by the threat of, or use of, force;

(5) **Theft and handling stolen goods** – including shoplifting, theft of cycles and stealing cars;

(6) **Fraud and forgery** – including fraud by a company director, false accounting, deception and forging prescriptions for drugs;

(7) **Criminal damage** – including arson and criminal damage endangering life and criminal damage of value £20 and under;

(8) **Other notifiable offences** – including blackmail, kidnapping, drugs offences, treason, libel, and absconding from custody.

As this summary shows, the offence categories cover crimes of a differing degree of seriousness and complexity; for example, violence against the person includes minor assault and murder.

Where forces use computerised crime-recording systems to extract the data for Home Office returns, it should be possible to take data on individual offence classifications and recategorise it in a format which is more useful for performance evaluation. Such categorisation would address two issues:

(i) *seriousness* – thus a multi-million-pound pension fraud would be categorised separately from a fraudulent DSS claim valued at £20;

(ii) *complexity of investigation* – for example, shoplifting is almost self-detecting since a likely suspect is apprehended at the point of commission of the offence. Some town centre BCUs have high overall primary detection rates because of the large number of shoplifting offences reported to them. Separating this offence allows for a more meaningful comparison of performance between BCUs.

POSSIBLE ALTERNATIVE GROUPINGS OF OFFENCES:

(1) **Murder**

(2) **Very serious crimes** – attempted murder, manslaughter, rape, wounding endangering life;

(3) **Serious crimes** – other wounding, unlawful sexual intercourse, arson, robbery, supplying controlled drugs;

(4) **Fraud by a company director and false accounting etc.**

(5) **Burglary of dwelling** – including aggravated burglary but not, where practicable, attempted burglary (i.e. a failed attempt to burgle);

(6) **Theft, other (non-dwelling) burglary, other fraud and forgery** – including handling stolen goods;

(7) **Vehicle crime** – theft of and from cars and aggravated vehicle-taking;

(8) **Shoplifting**

(9) **Other crimes – including attempted burglary.**

This categorisation, whilst far from perfect – the category of robbery, for example, still includes crimes with very differing degrees of violence – would offer managers better insights into relative workload and performance. However, there will always be pressure to produce a 'headline figure' describing overall performance rather than quoting eight or nine clear-up figures.

This point could be addressed by assigning weightings to each category so that detection of a murder or a rape was not equated with a caution for shoplifting. Several factors could be taken into account to determine weightings: seriousness, average time taken to investigate, historic clear-up performance and professional assessments by experienced detectives of the relative difficulty of investigation. The highest weightings would be given to the force's highest priorities, providing a yardstick for senior management to use to measure the force's overall success in meeting its specified objectives.

It is unlikely that such a weighting process will ever be totally scientific; the question for managers is whether it offers a better basis for comparative evaluation than current approaches.